AF575934

SOUTHERN OREGON

BARBARA TRICARICO

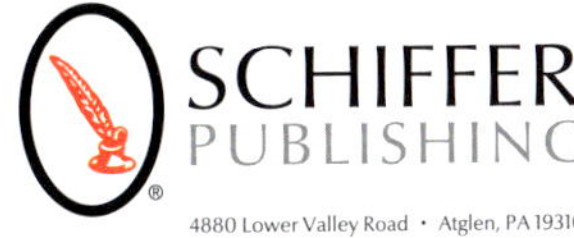

4880 Lower Valley Road • Atglen, PA 19310

Other Schiffer Books by Barbara Tricarico:

Oregon, ISBN 978-0-7643-5946-0
Oregon Coast, ISBN 978-0-7643-5947-7
Central Oregon, ISBN 978-0-7643-5945-3
Ashland, Oregon Day Trips, ISBN 978-0-7643-5014-6
Ashland, Oregon, ISBN 978-0-7643-4490-9

Library of Congress Control Number: 2019947457

Designed by Molly Shields
Cover photo by Jim Craven
Back cover photos, clockwise from left: Jay Newman, Jay Newman, Terry Fisher, John Christer Petersen

Type set in BentonSans/Cambria

ISBN: 978-0-7643-5948-4
Printed in China

Published by Schiffer Publishing, Ltd.
4880 Lower Valley Road
Atglen, PA 19310
Phone: (610) 593-1777; Fax: (610) 593-2002
E-mail: Info@schifferbooks.com
Web: www.schifferbooks.com

INTRODUCTION

Southern Oregon is surrounded by natural beauty in a postcard-perfect setting. Crater Lake is Oregon's only national park and is often called one of the Seven Natural Wonders of the World. The Rogue, Umpqua, Illinois, and Christmas Valleys dip beneath the Cascade and Siskiyou mountain ranges, providing profuse hiking trails, lakes, streams, and scenery.

There are many artsy towns, such as Ashland, which draws visitors to the Oregon Shakespeare Festival, Lithia Park, and the Mount Ashland ski resort. Throughout Southern Oregon, including the lush Applegate River Valley, there are countless wineries to visit. The former gold-rush town of Jacksonville has history, charm, and art. Cave Junction's motto is "Gateway to the Oregon Caves," with more than 4,554 acres to explore.

Grants Pass is a hub of activity for the Rogue River, with whitewater rafting, fishing, camping, hiking, and plentiful nature and wildlife along its banks. There is an abundance of other water activity in Southern Oregon, including Lake of the Woods, Hyatt Lake, Howard Prairie Lake, Emigrant Lake, Lake Selmac, and Diamond Lake. The vibrant blue-green Illinois River also provides a variety of water experiences. Venture into the Umpqua River Valley (not far from Crater Lake) and explore countless distinctive waterfalls.

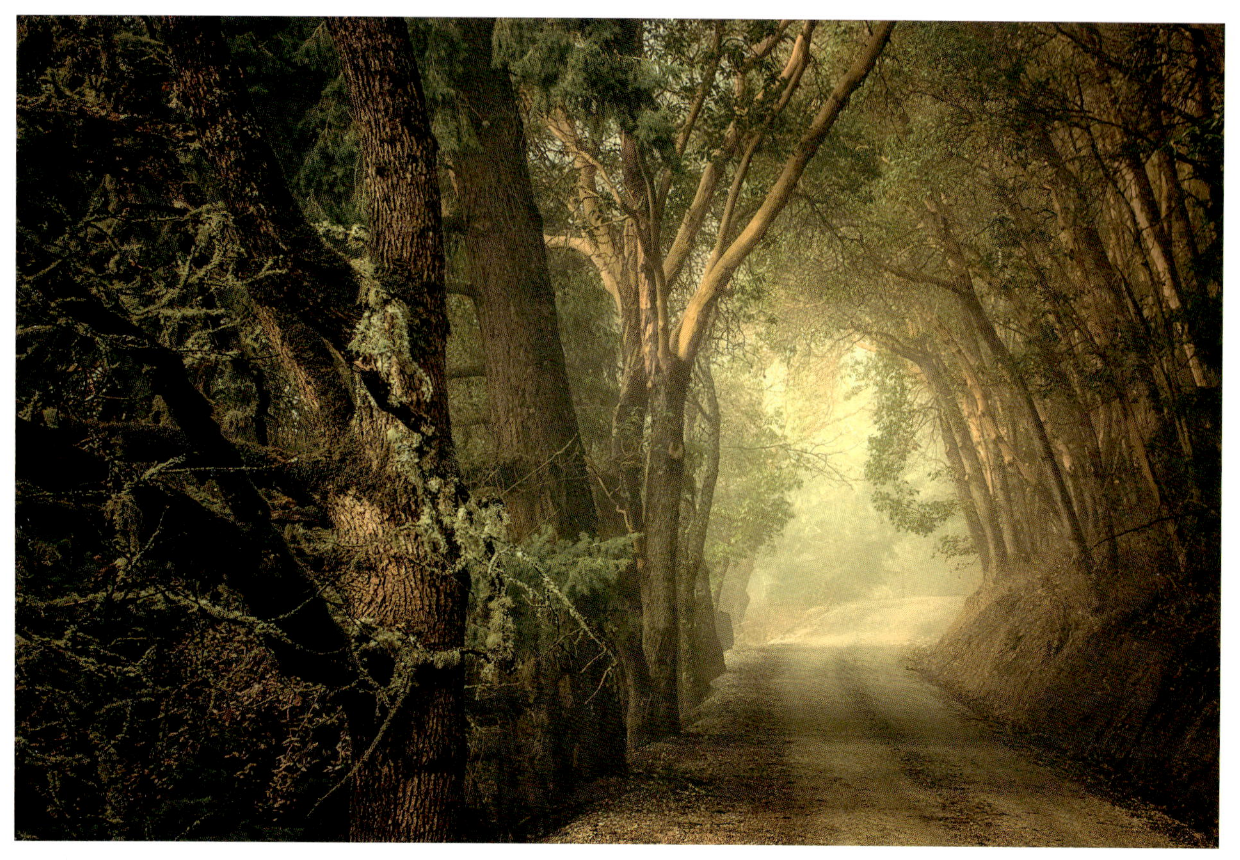

 Talent, Oregon. *Photo by David Lorenz Winston.*

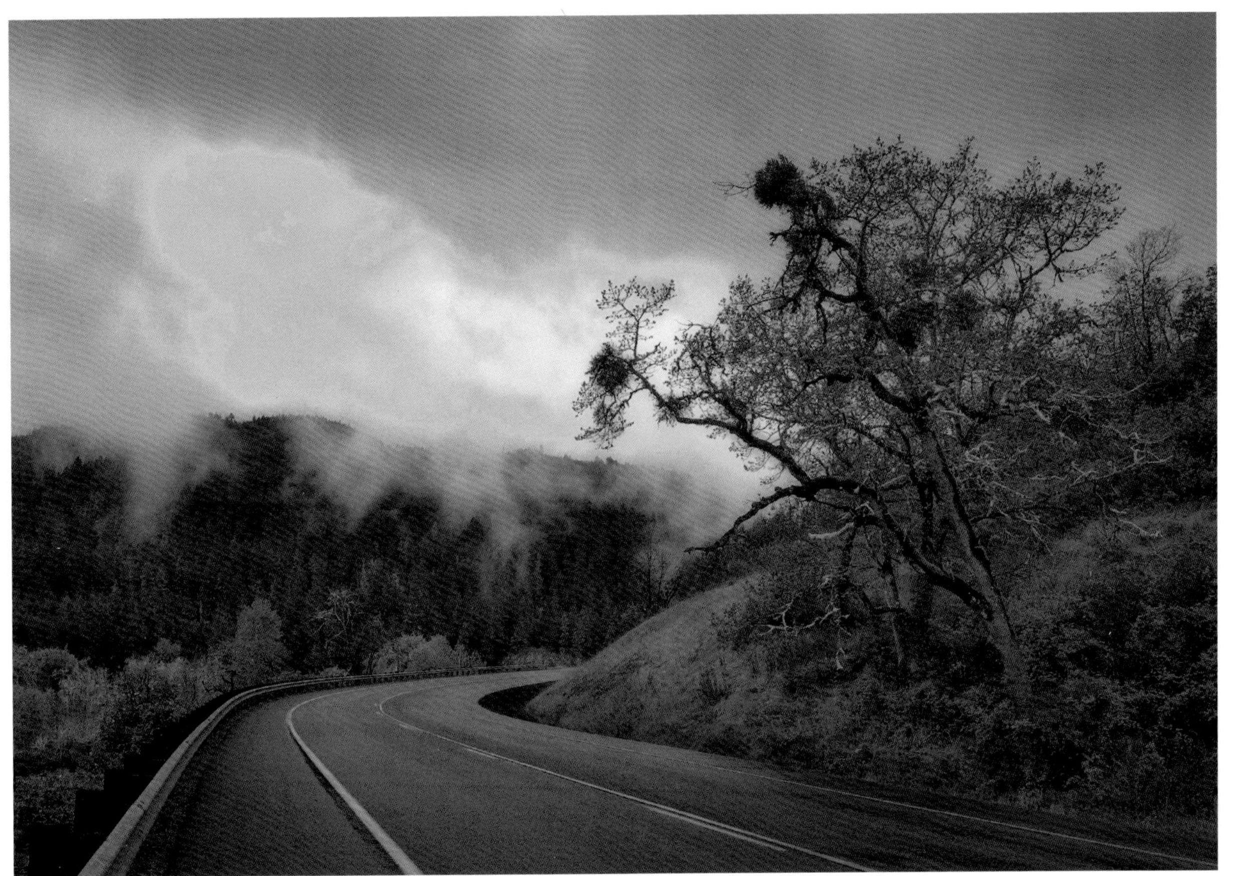

Fog on Umpqua Highway. *Photo by John Christer Petersen.*

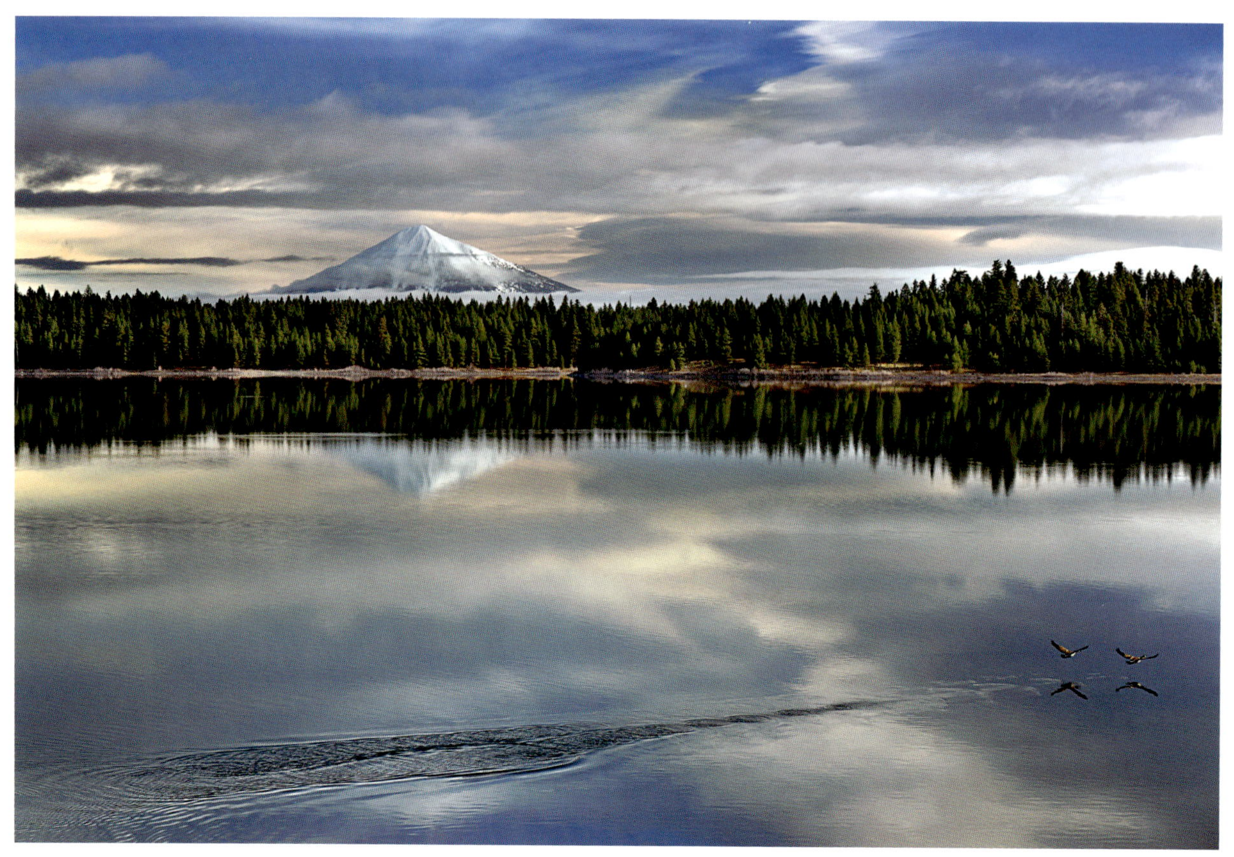

 Howard Prairie Lake and Mount McLaughlin. *Photo by Jim Craven.*

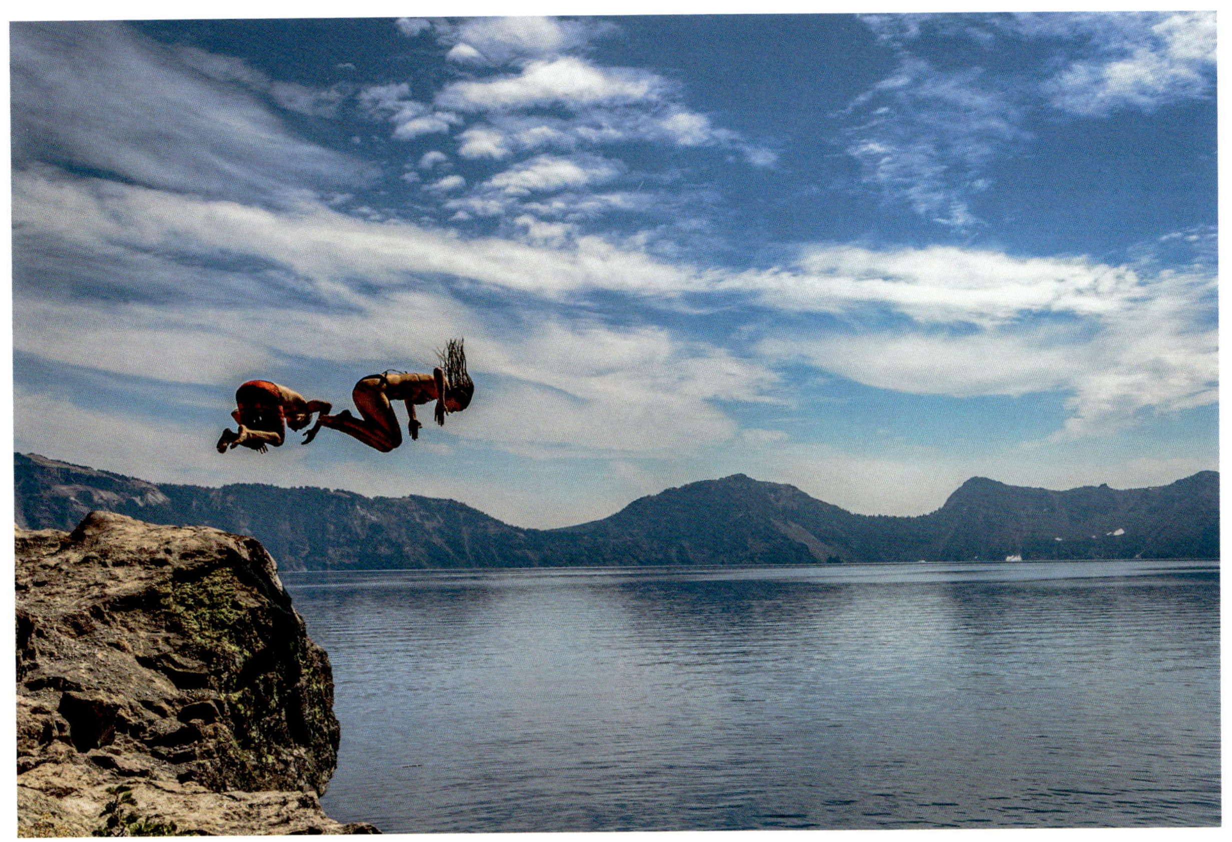

Crater Lake Dive. *Photo by Nick Viani.*

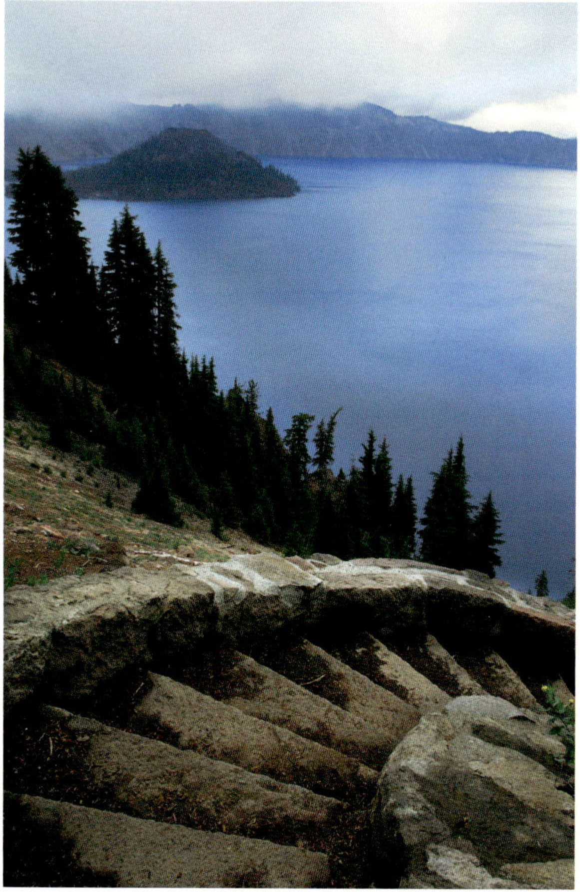

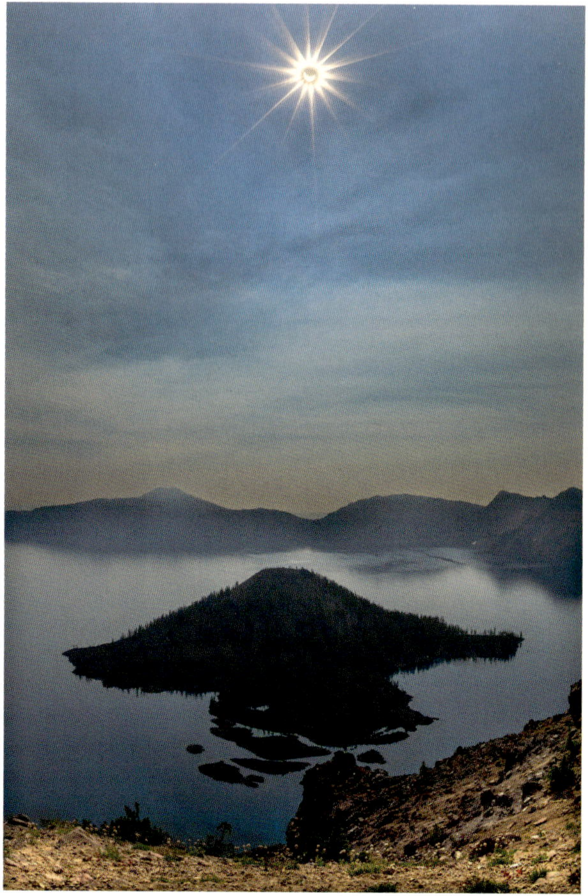

 Crater Lake steps. *Photo by Jay Newman.* • Solar eclipse over Wizard Island, Crater Lake. *Photo by Sue Newman.*

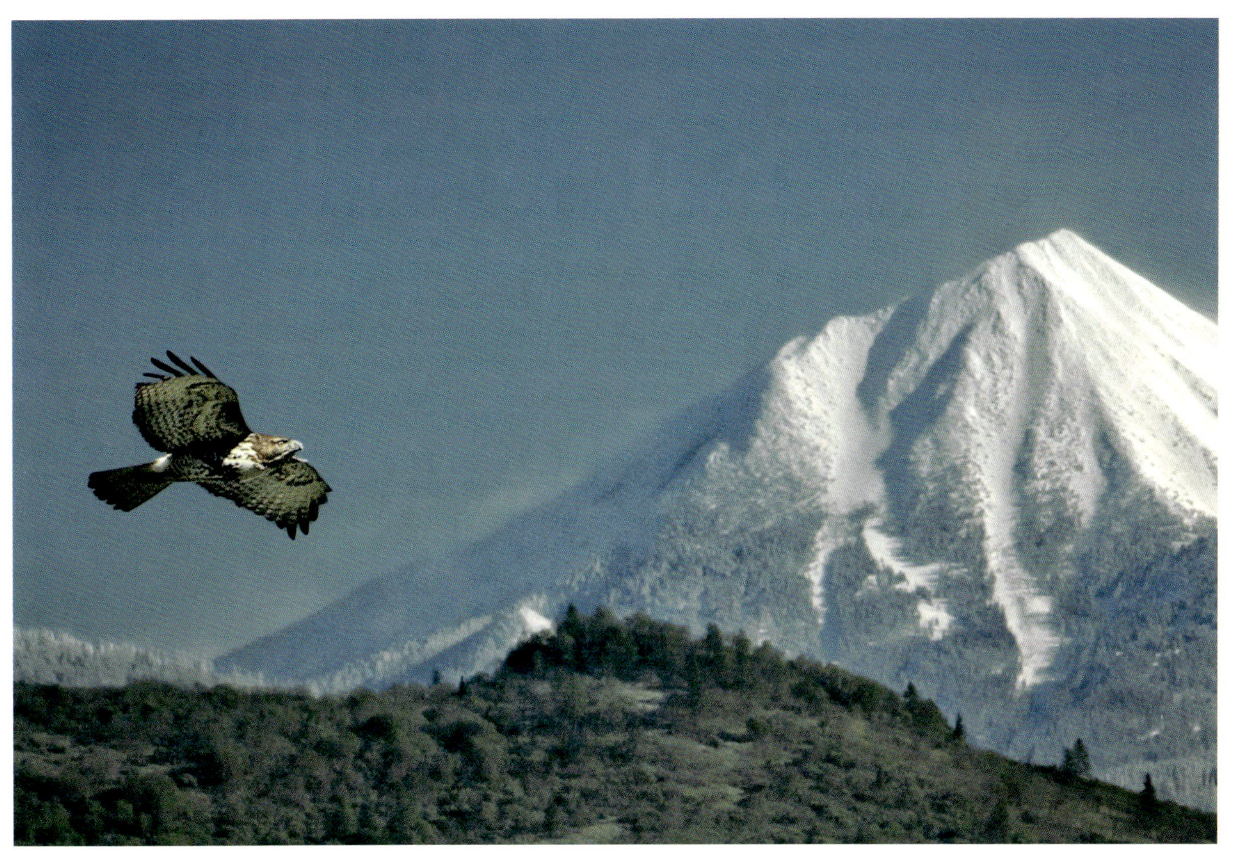

Red-tailed hawk at Mount McLoughlin. *Photo by Matt Witt.*

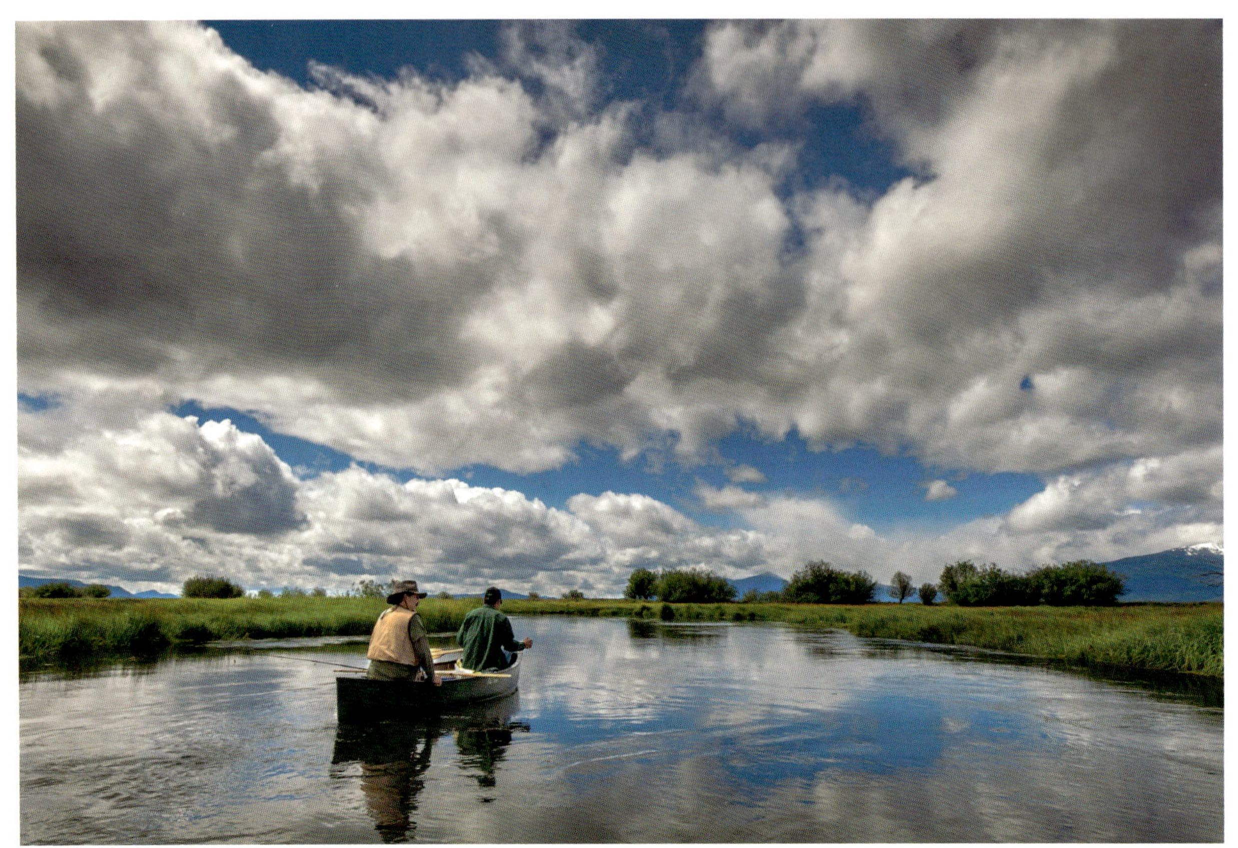

 Wood River. *Photo by Jim Craven.*

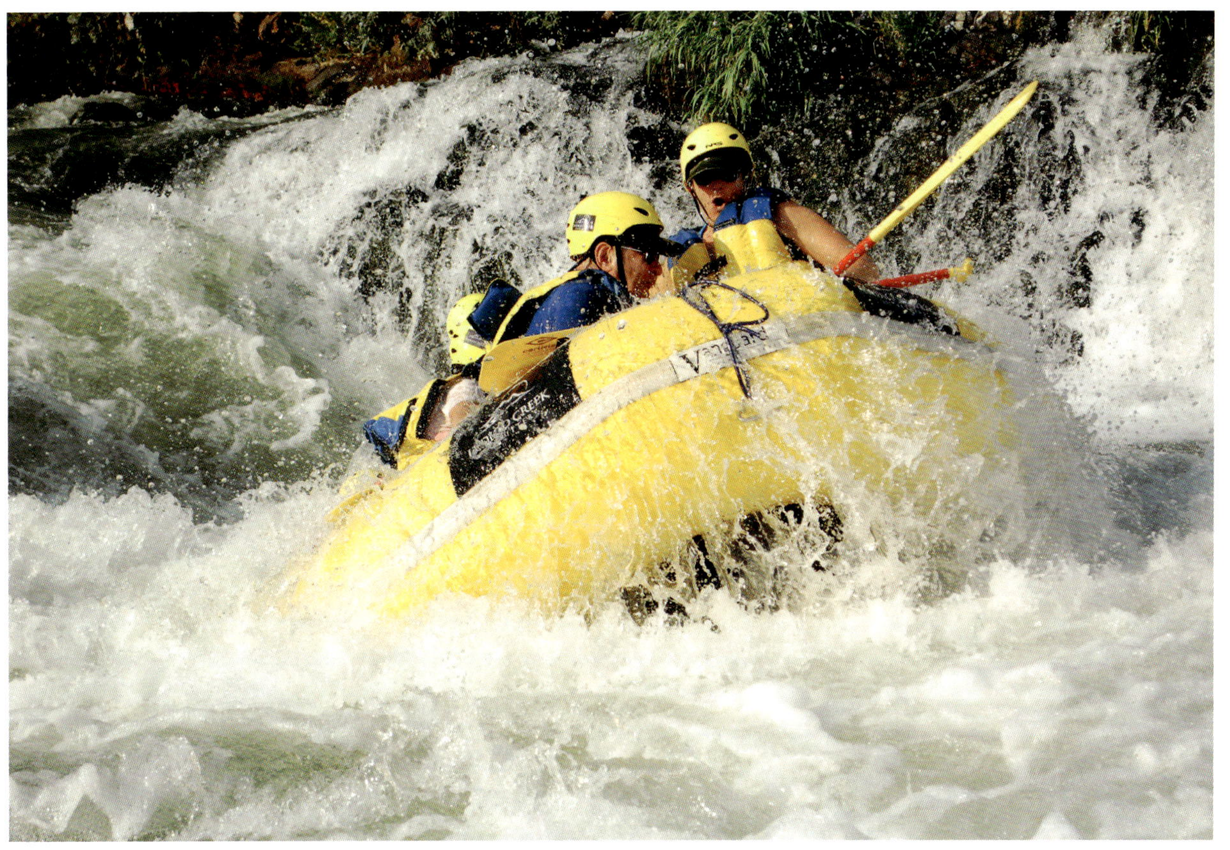

Rafting on Powerhouse Rapids through Ti'lomikh Falls on the Rogue River. *Photo by Will Volpert, Indigo Creek Outfitters.*

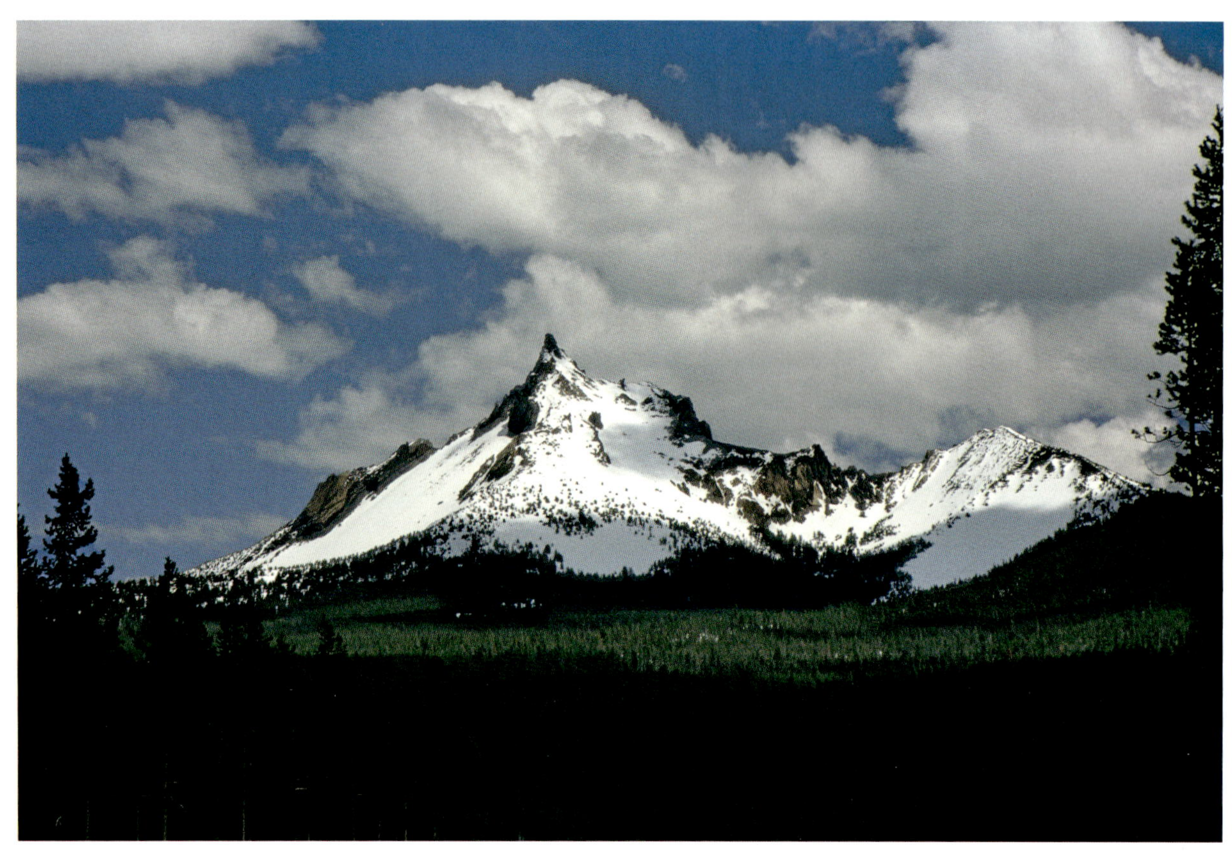

 Mount Thielsen. *Photo by Nomeca Hartwell.*

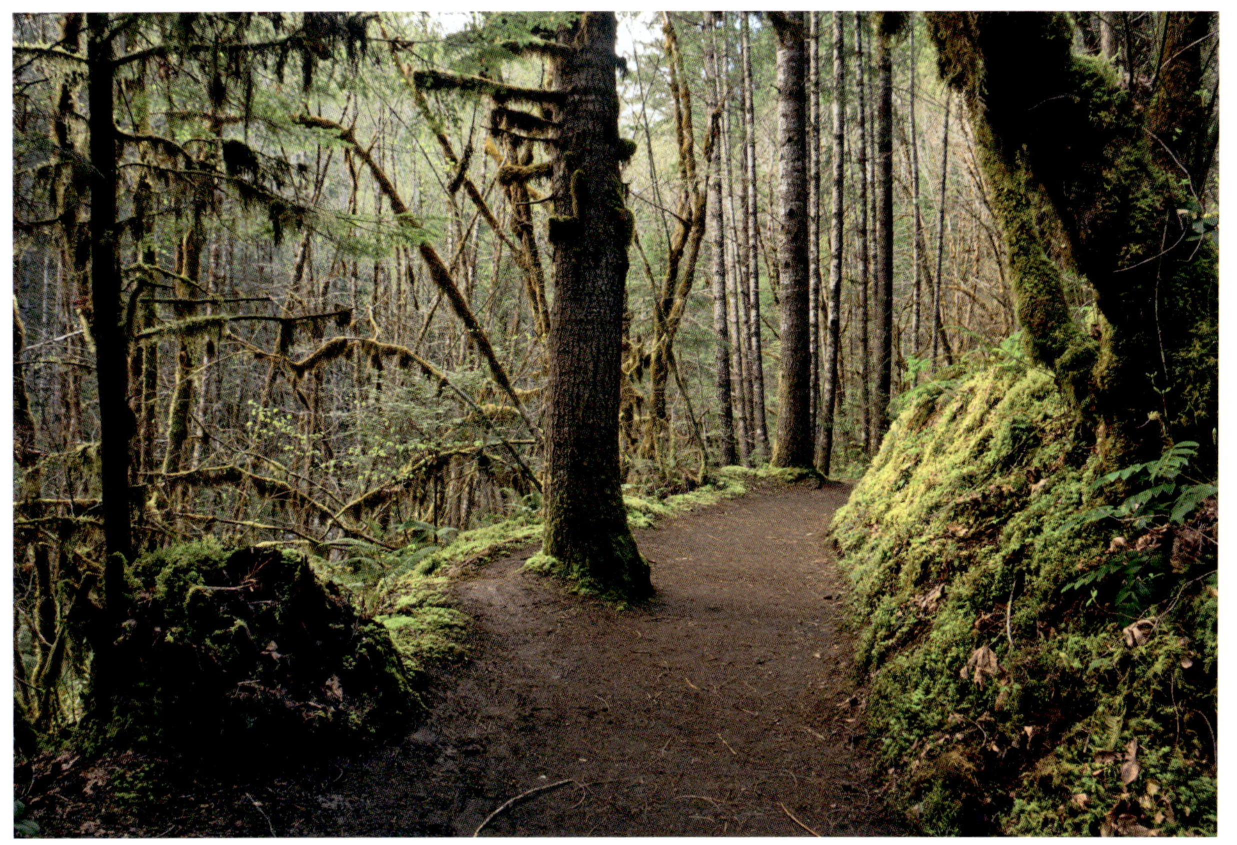

Susan Creek Falls Trail, Umpqua National Forest. *Photo by Jay Newman.*

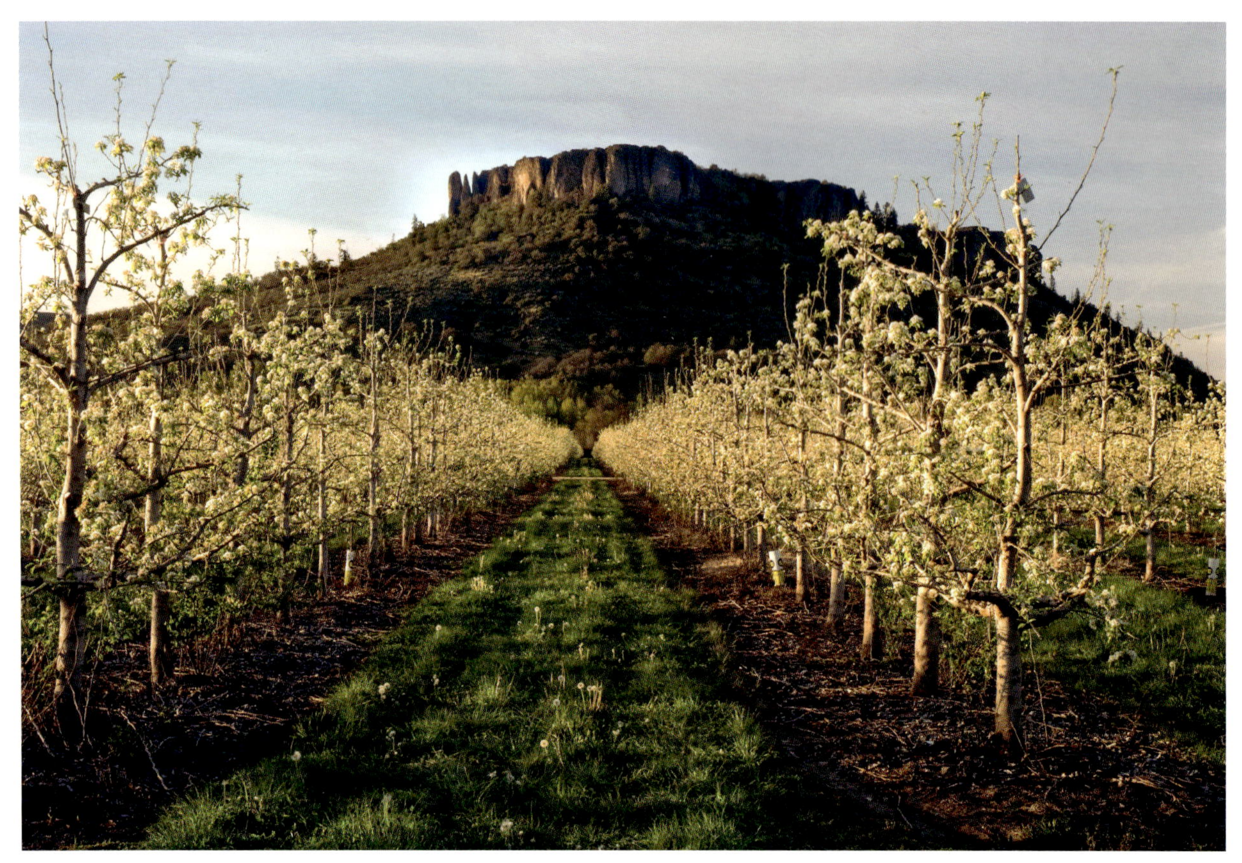

 Lower Table Rock and orchards, Central Point. *Photo by Jay Newman.*

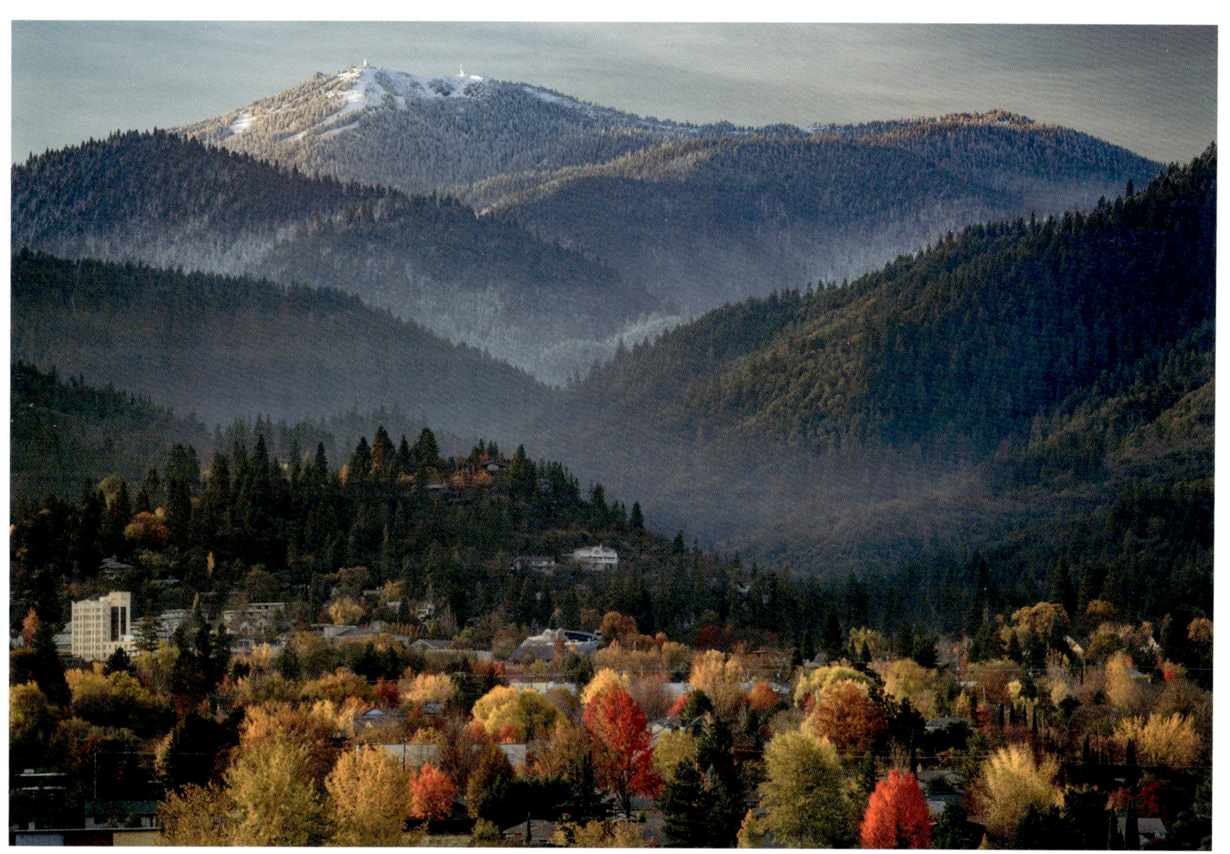

Ashland in the fall, with Mount Ashland in the background. *Photo by Sean Bagshaw.*

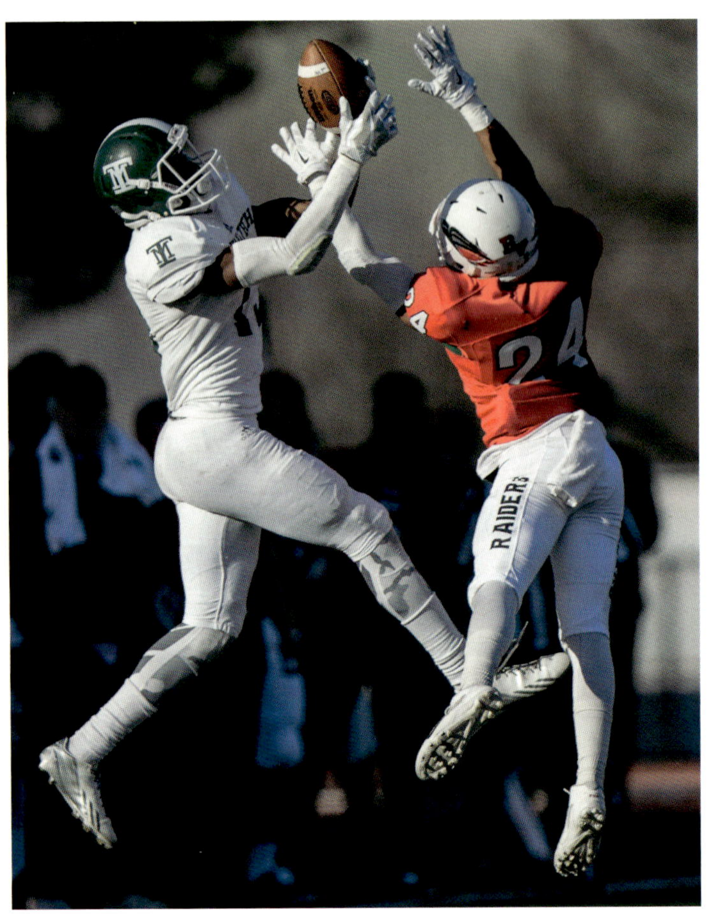

 Southern Oregon University Raiders football, Ashland. *Photo by Bob Palermini.*

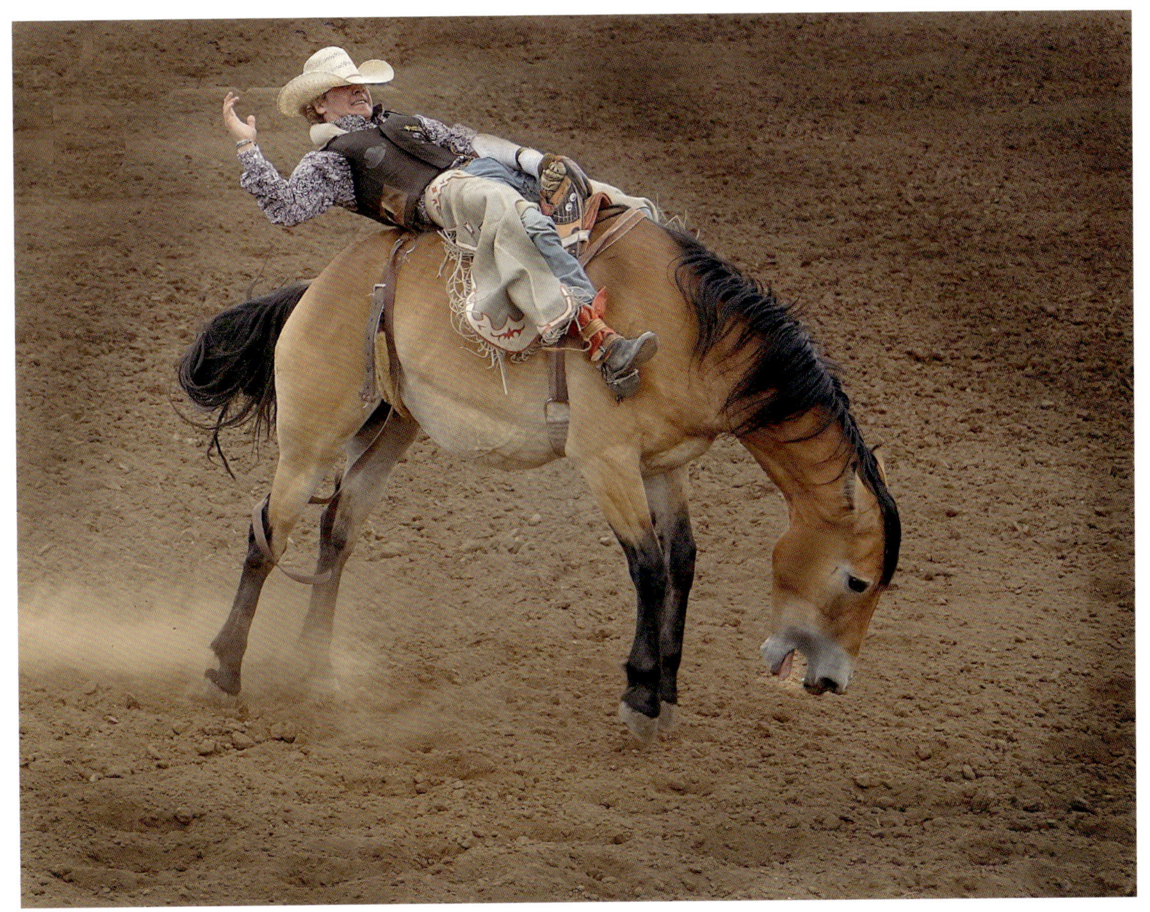

Canyonville Rodeo. *Photo by Neal R. Thompson.*

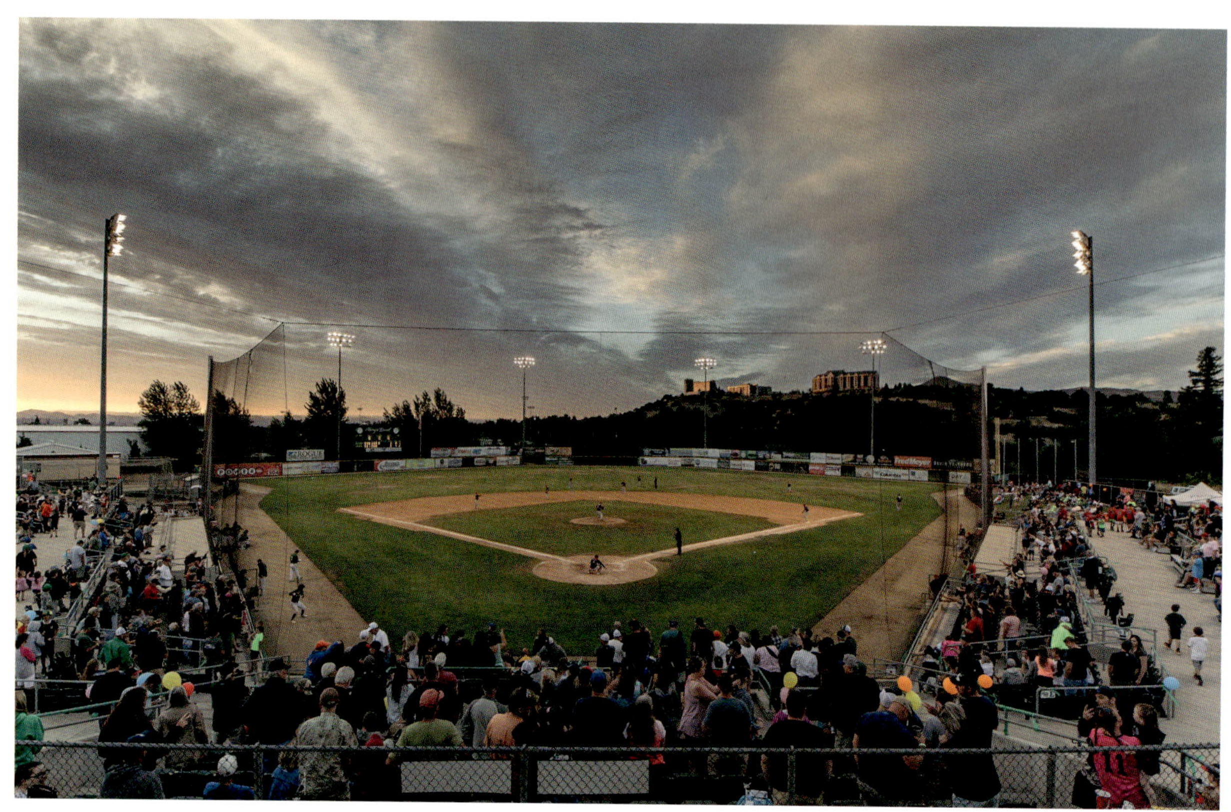

 Medford Rogues baseball at Harry and David Field. *Photo by Bob Palermini.*

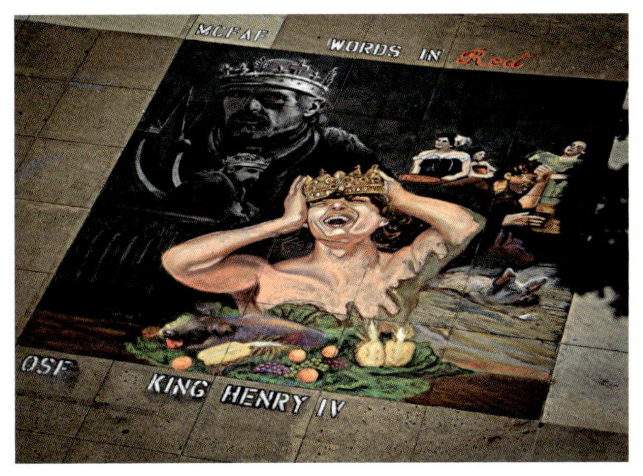

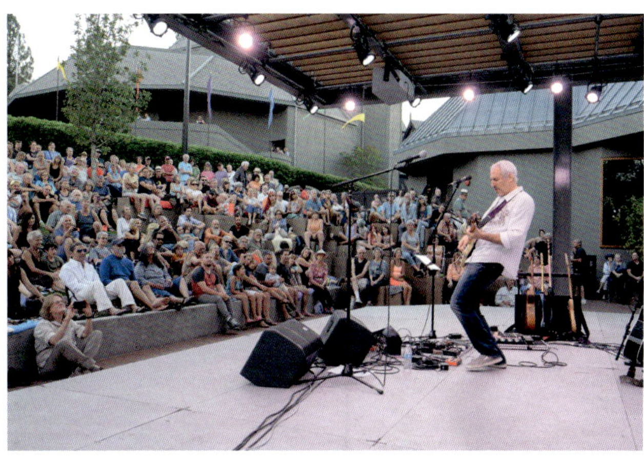

King Henry IV chalk painting in front of Oregon Shakespeare Festival's Black Swan Theatre, by artist Cathy Gallatin. *Photo by Graham Lewis.*

Oregon Shakespeare Festival Green Show. *Photo by Bob Palermini.*

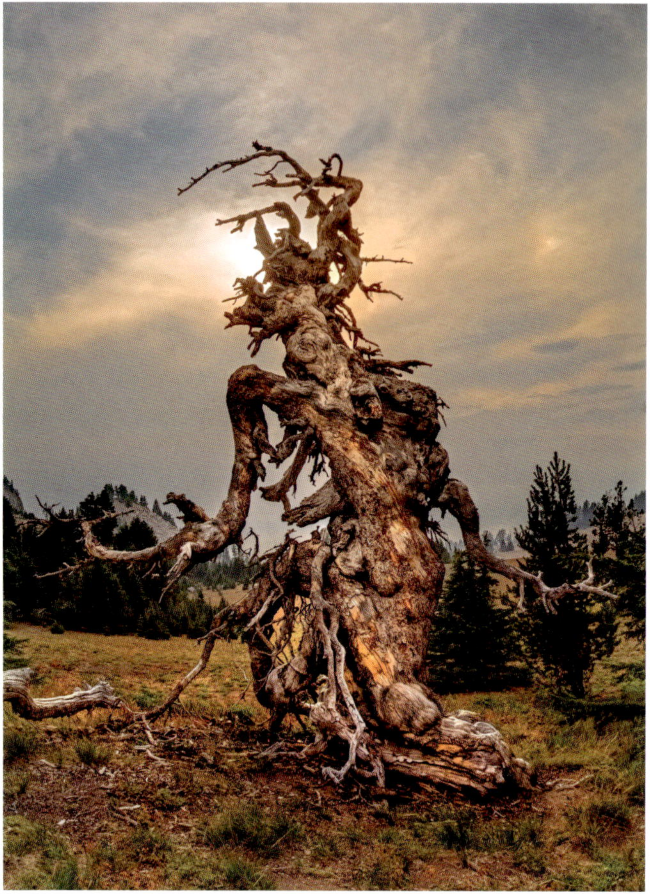

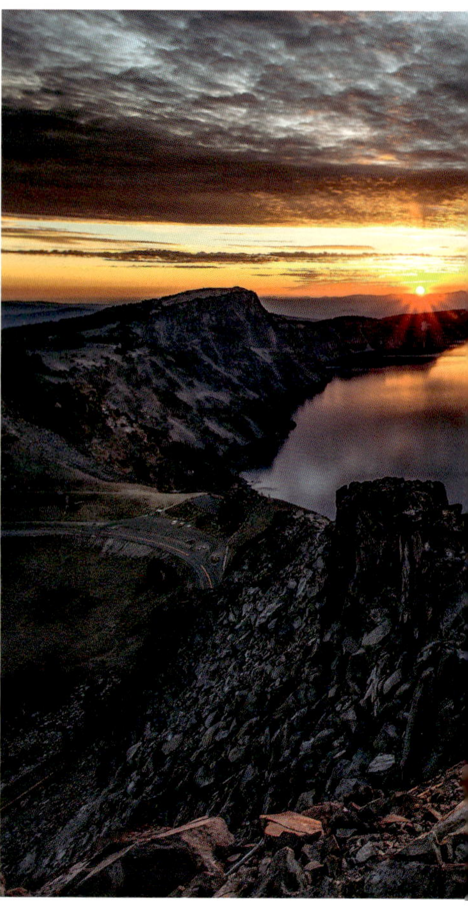

The Goddess Tree across from Watchman Peak trailhead, Crater Lake. *Photo by Sue Newman.*

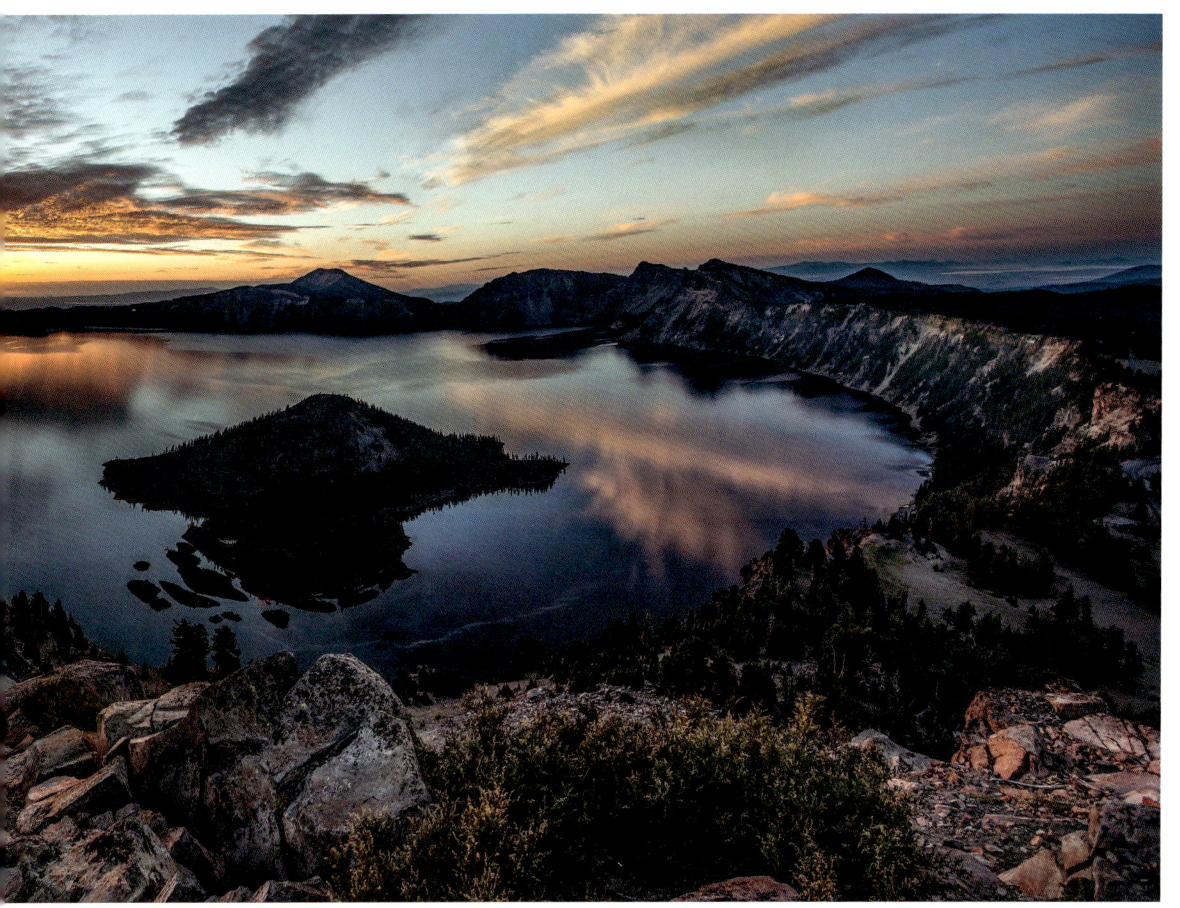

Crater Lake at sunrise. *Photo by Neal R. Thompson.*

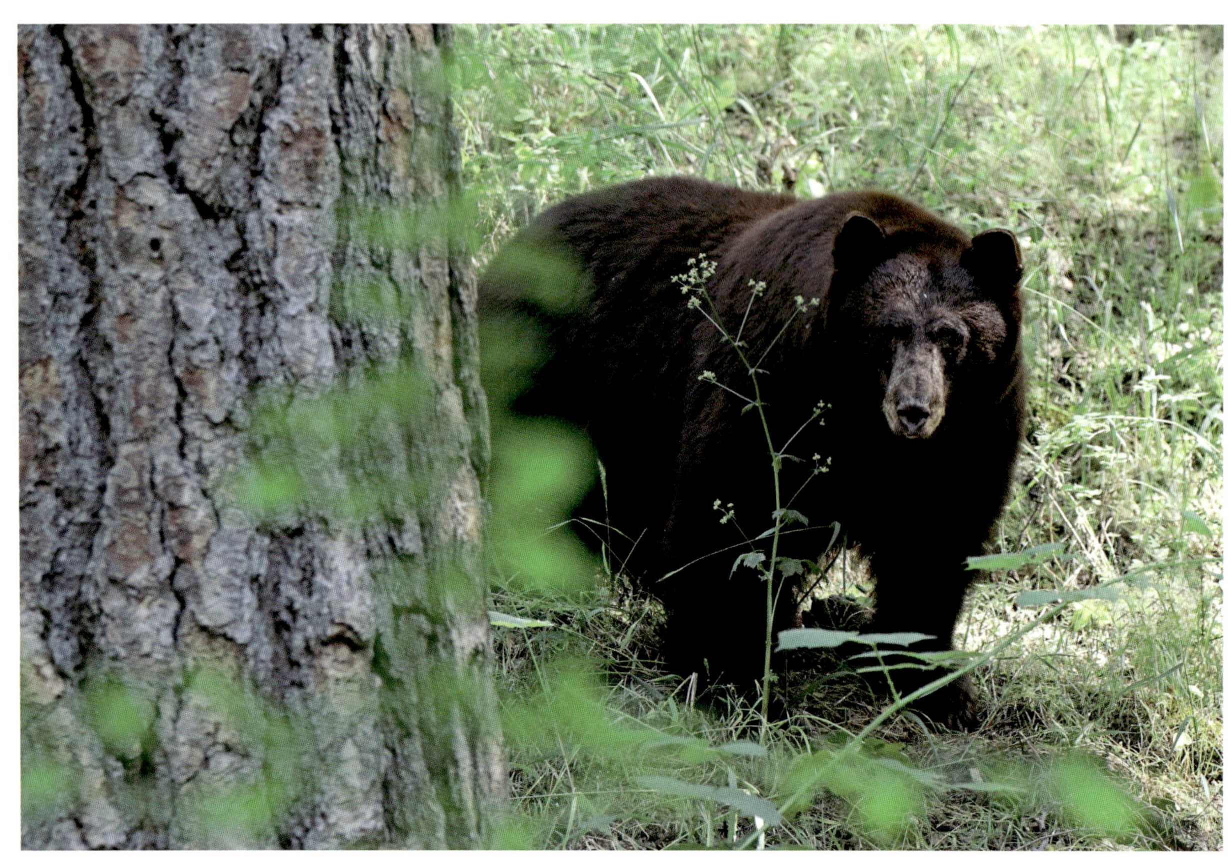

 Black bear. *Photo by Dan Elster.*

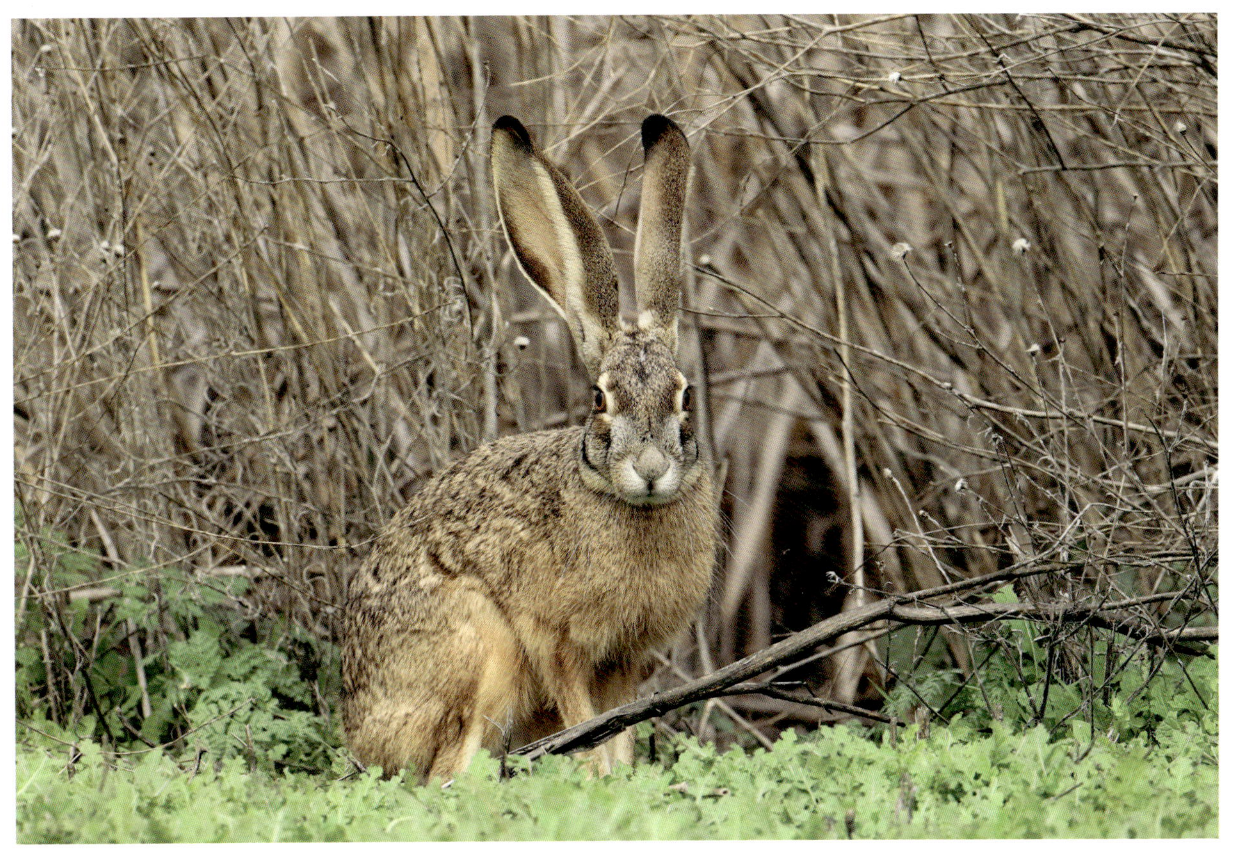

Black-tailed jackrabbit. *Photo by Dan Elster.*

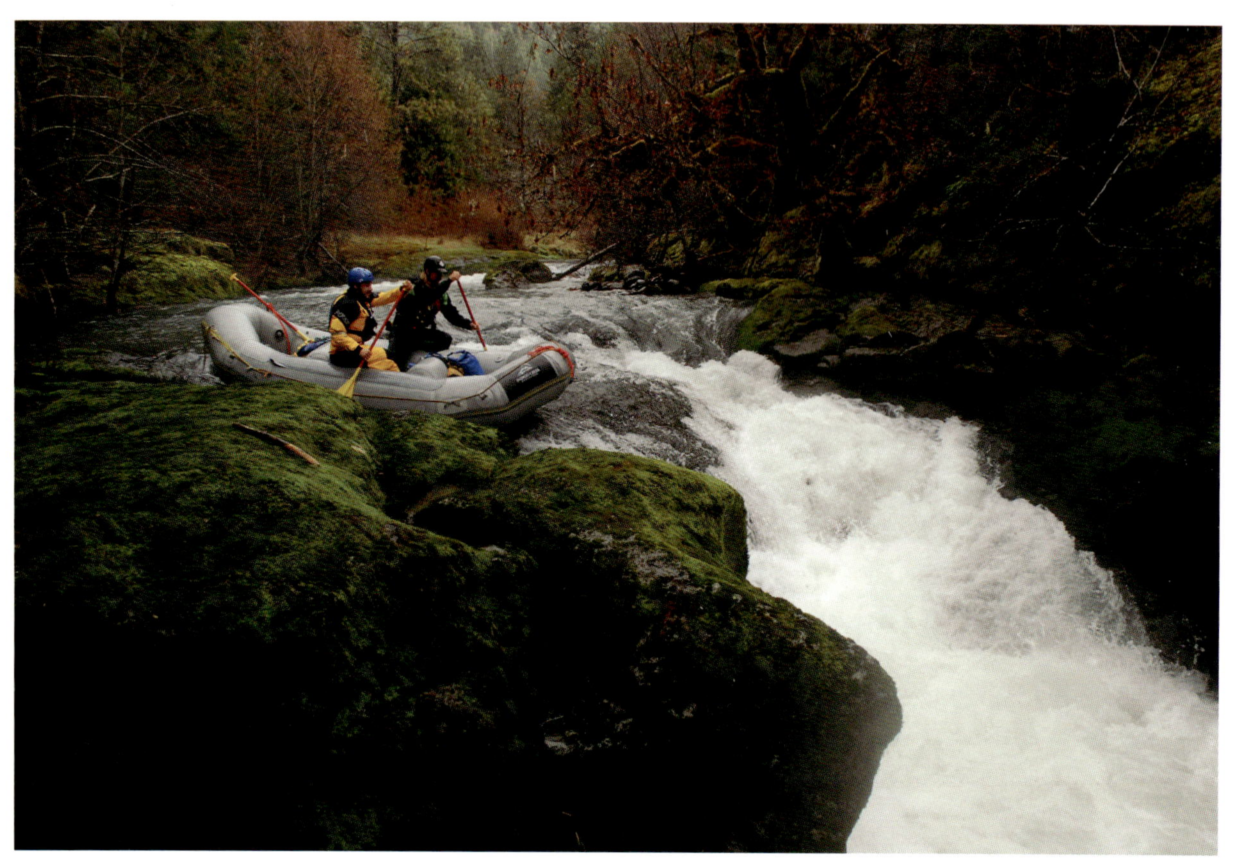

Rafting at Jackson Creek, a tributary of the South Umpqua River. *Photo by Will Volpert, Indigo Creek Outfitters.*

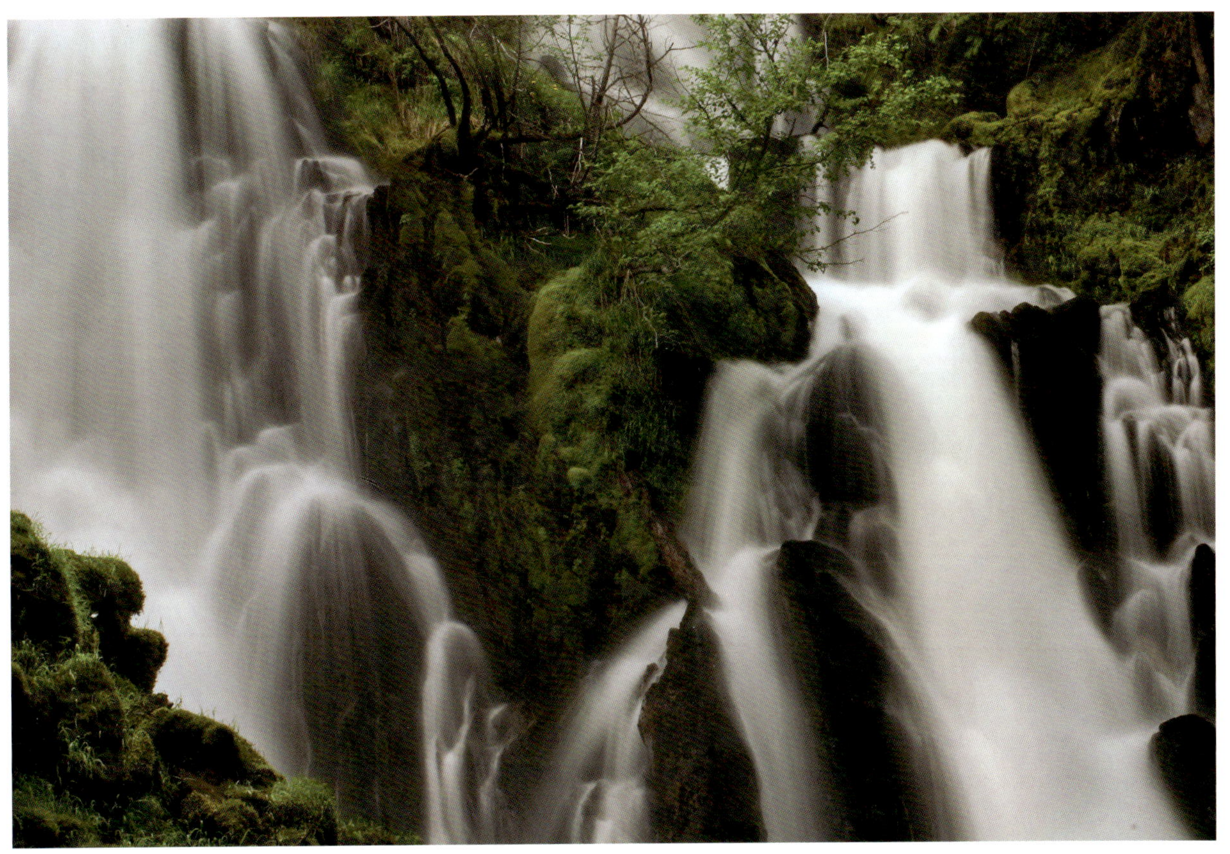

National Creek Falls near Crater Lake. *Photo by Jay Newman.*

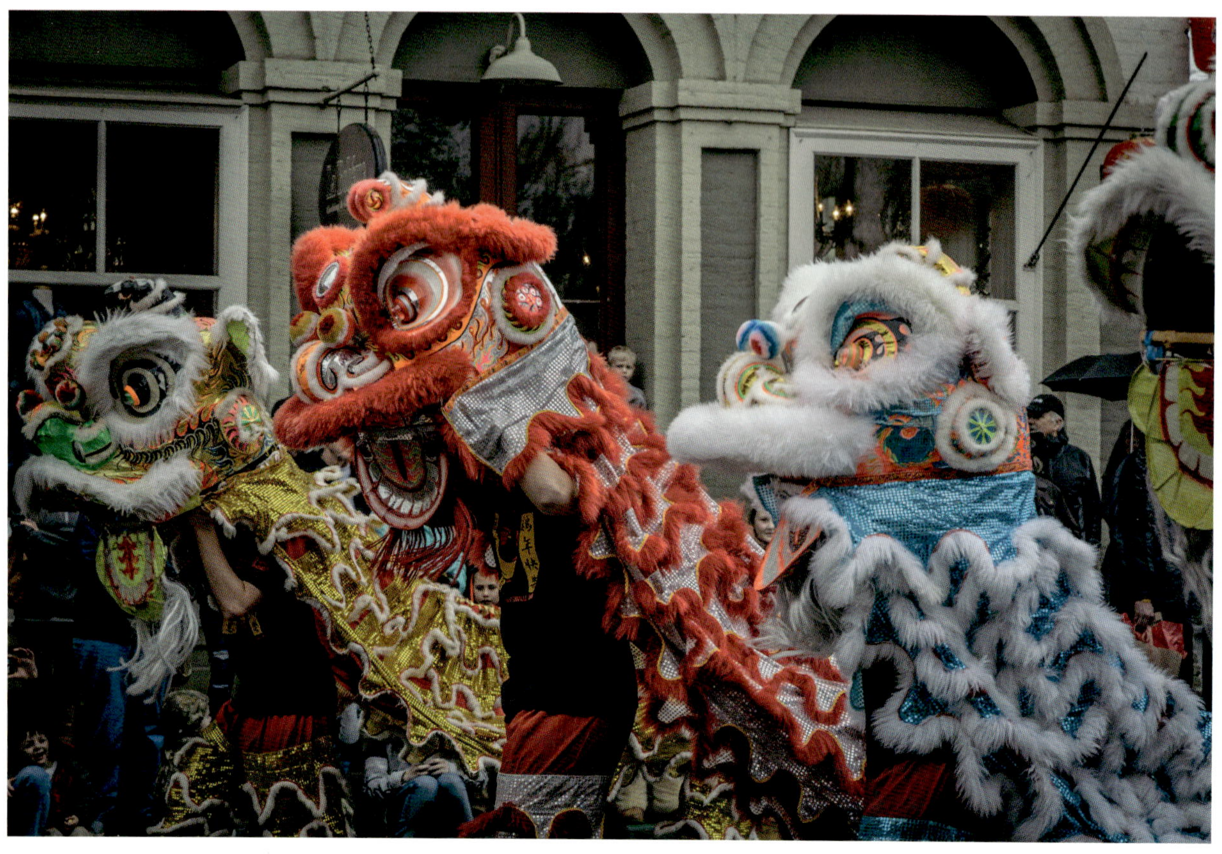

 Jacksonville's Chinese New Year Parade, celebrating the historic contributions of the Chinese in the region. *Photo by Alana Lynn Starkweather.*

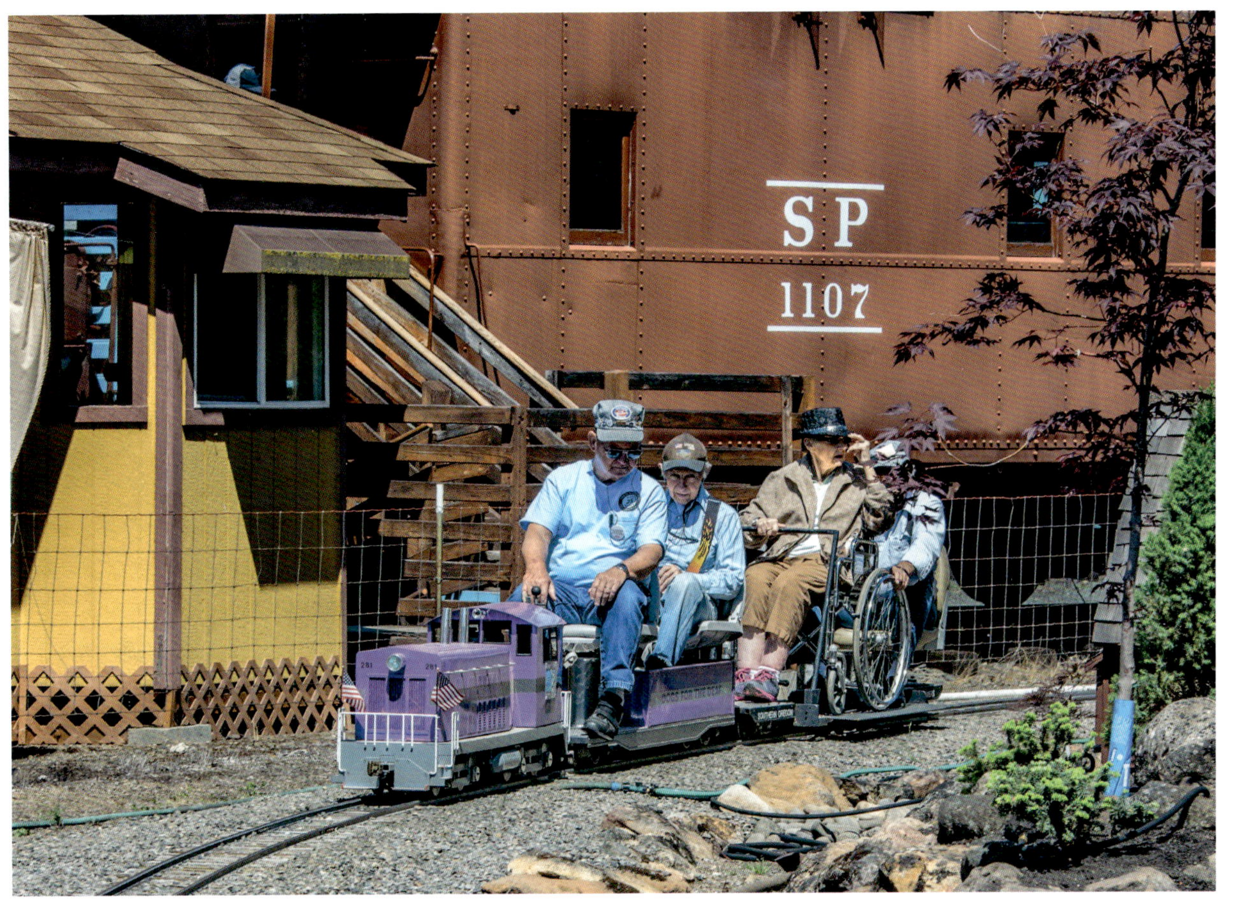

Medford Railroad Park. *Photo by George F. Peterson.*

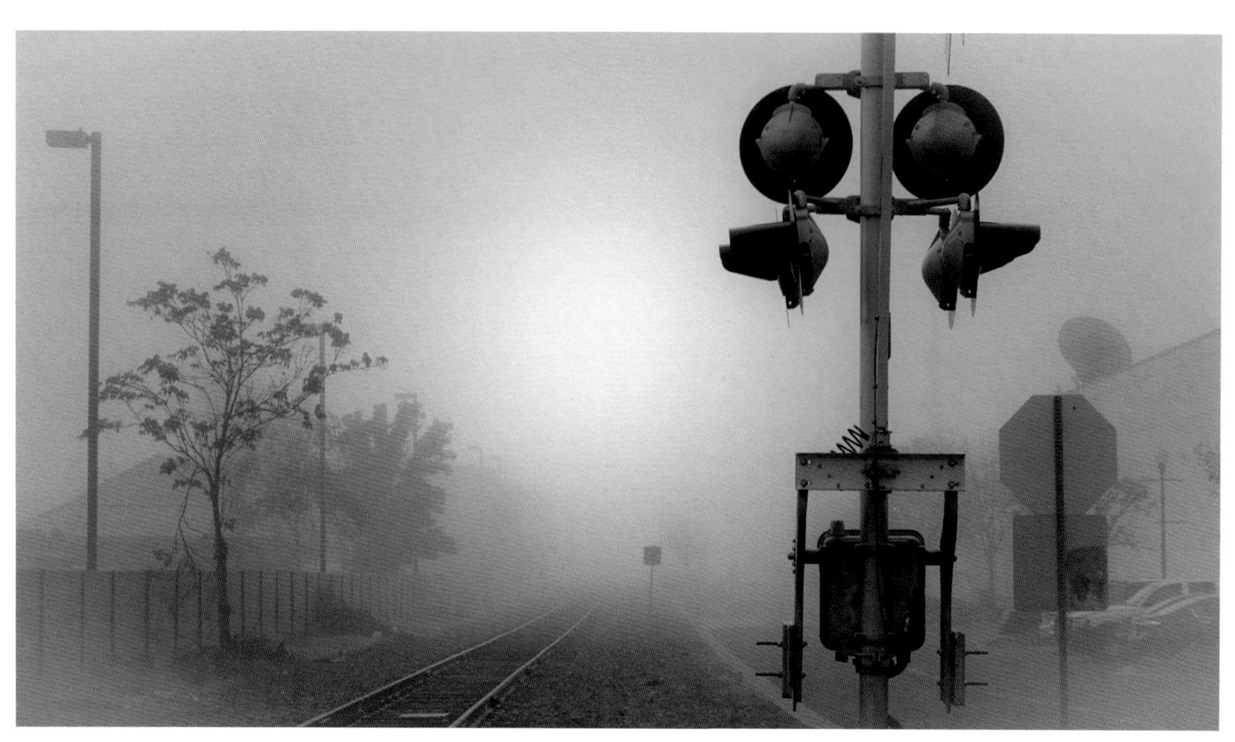

 Railroad tracks in Medford. *Photo by Atana Morell.*

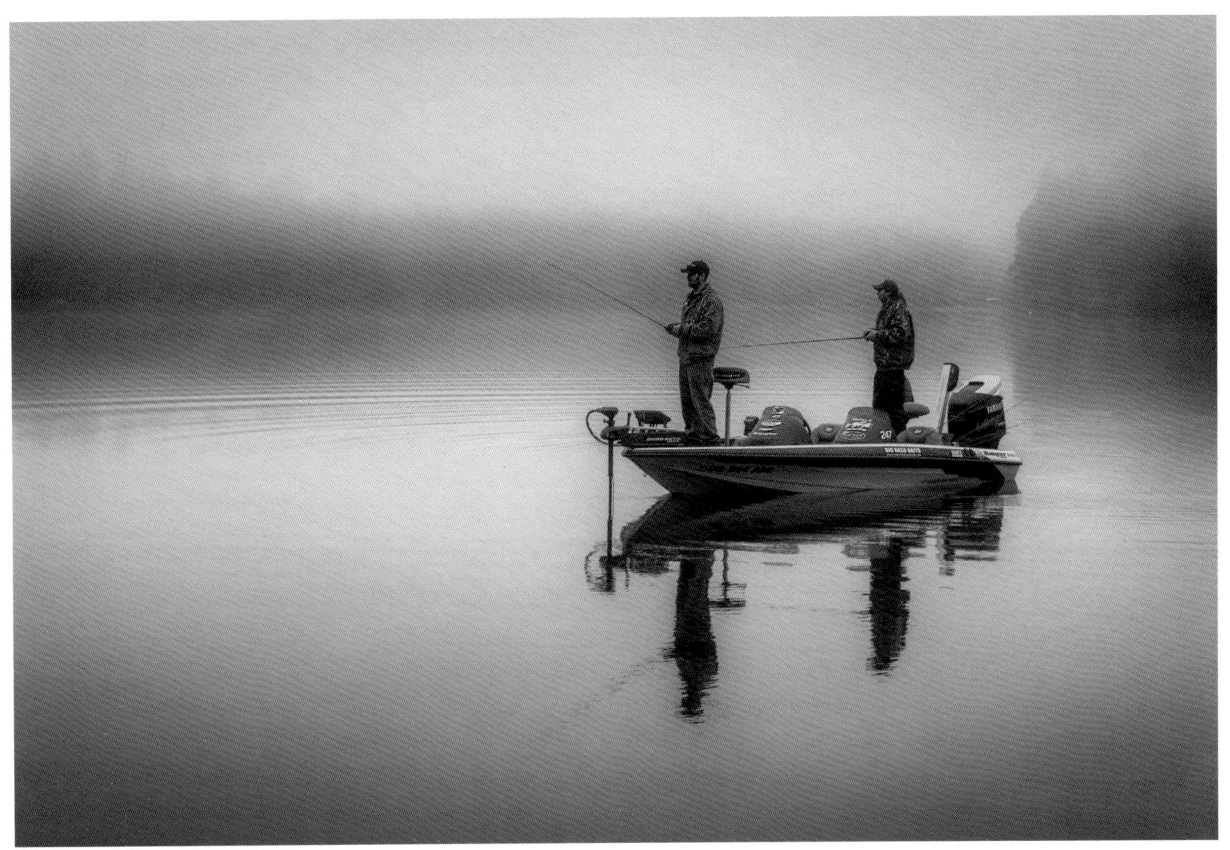

Fishing on Lake Selmac. *Photo by Barbara Tricarico.*

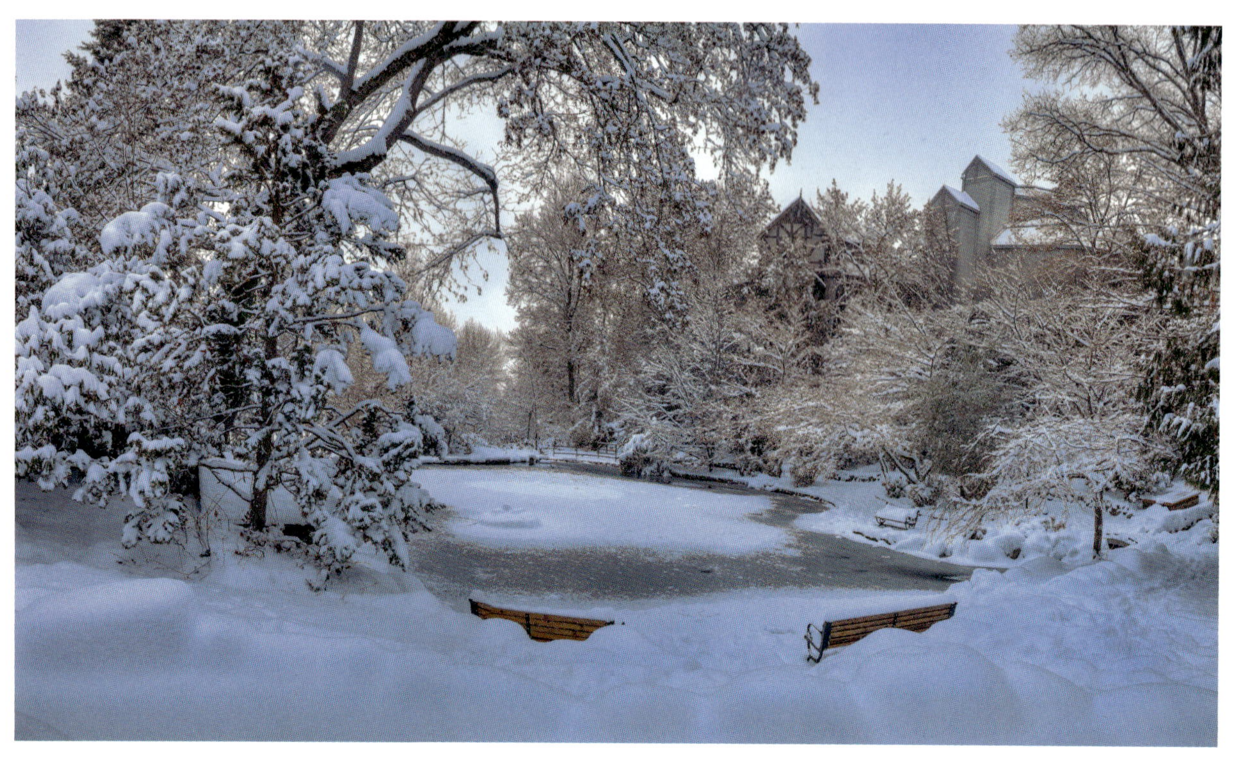

 Lithia Park's Lower Duck Pond, with Oregon Shakespeare Festival's Elizabethan Theatre in background, Ashland. *Photo by Neal R. Thompson.*

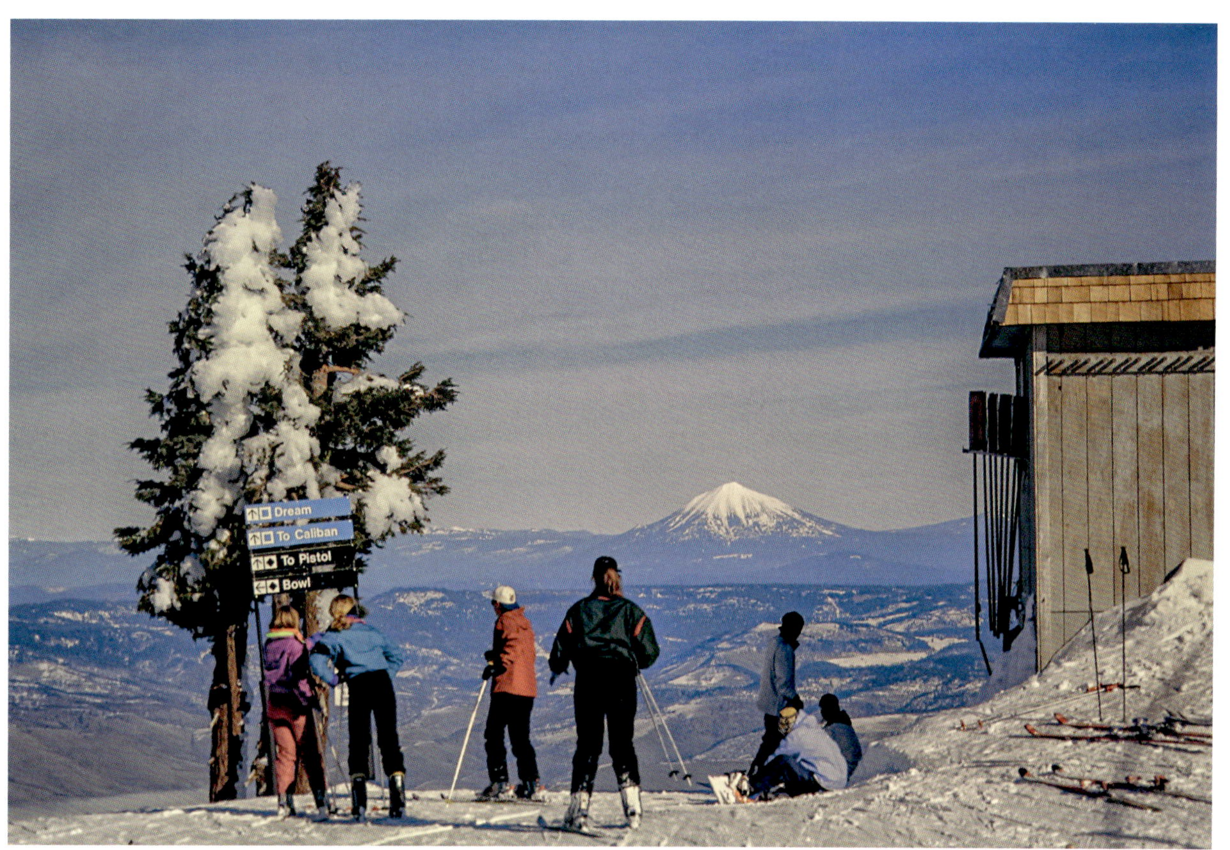

Mount Ashland skiers, with Mount Shasta in the distance. *Photo by Ken Deveney.*

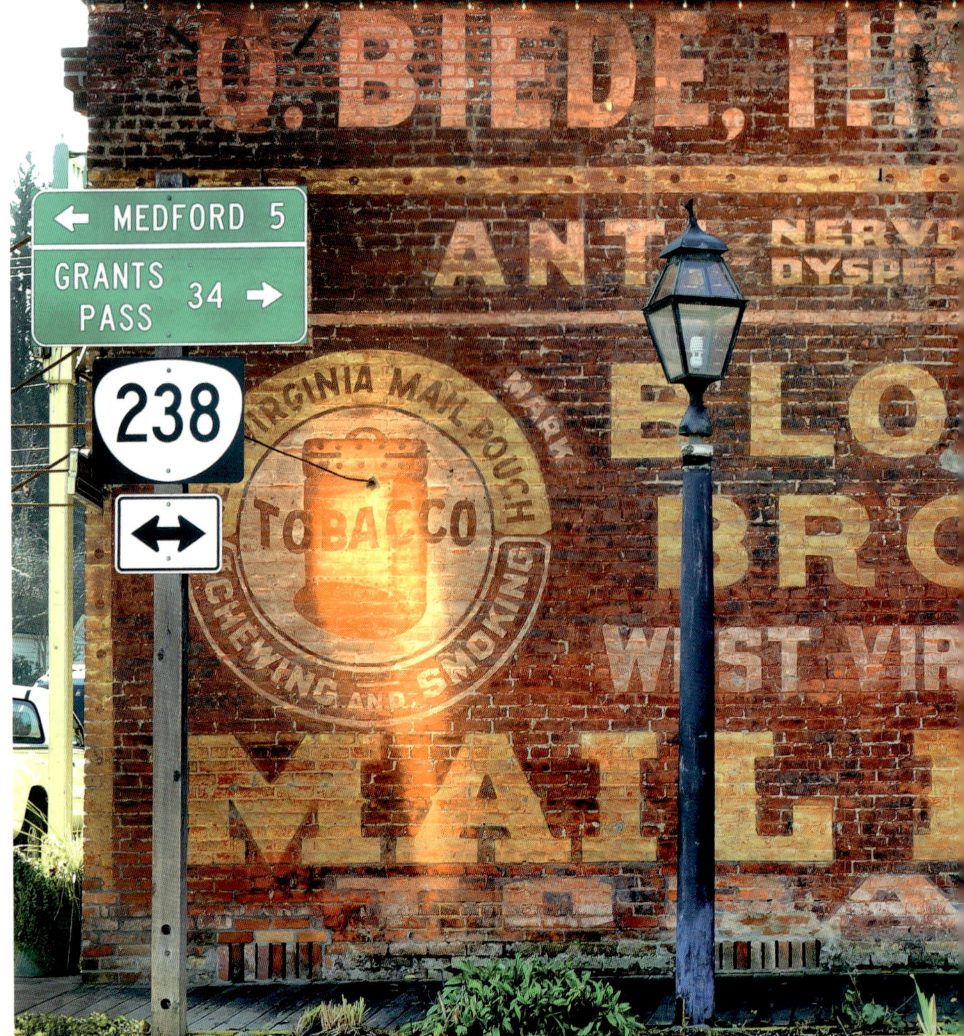

Jacksonville mural.
Photo by Jim Craven.

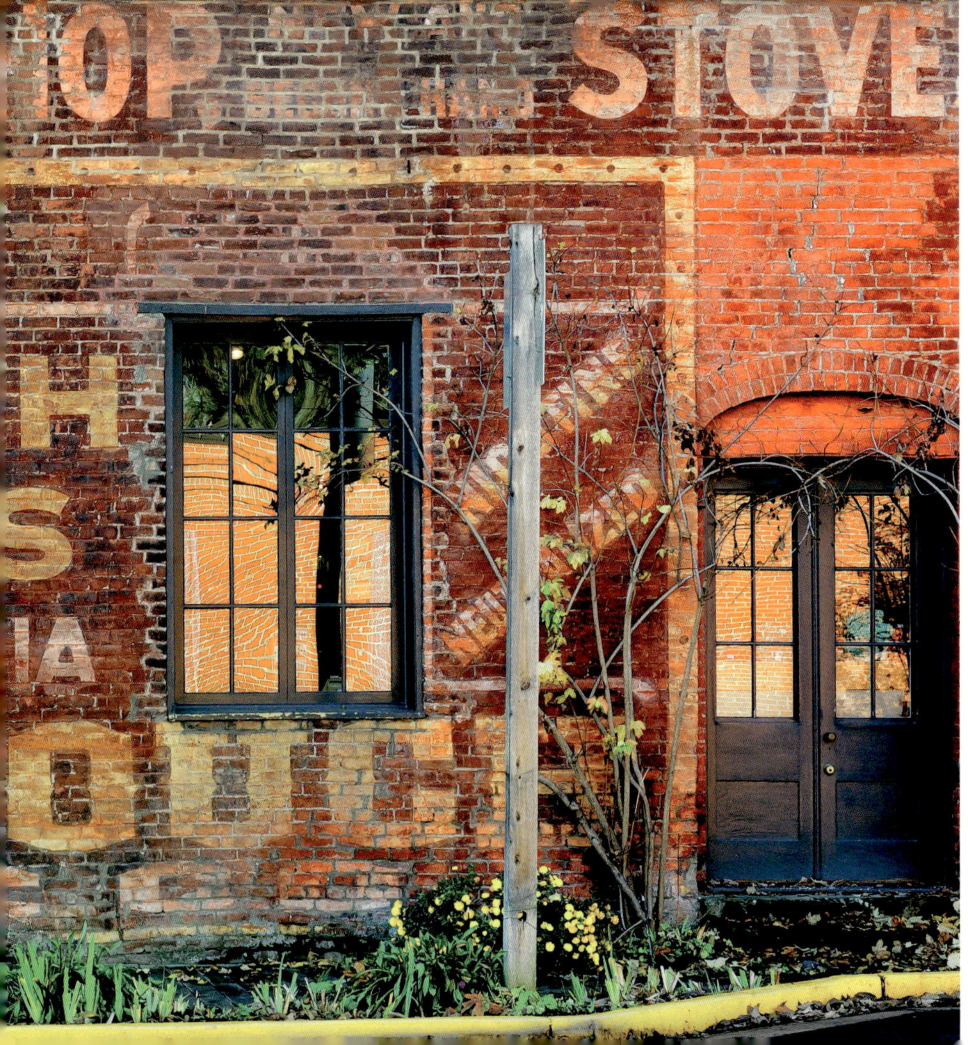
STOVE

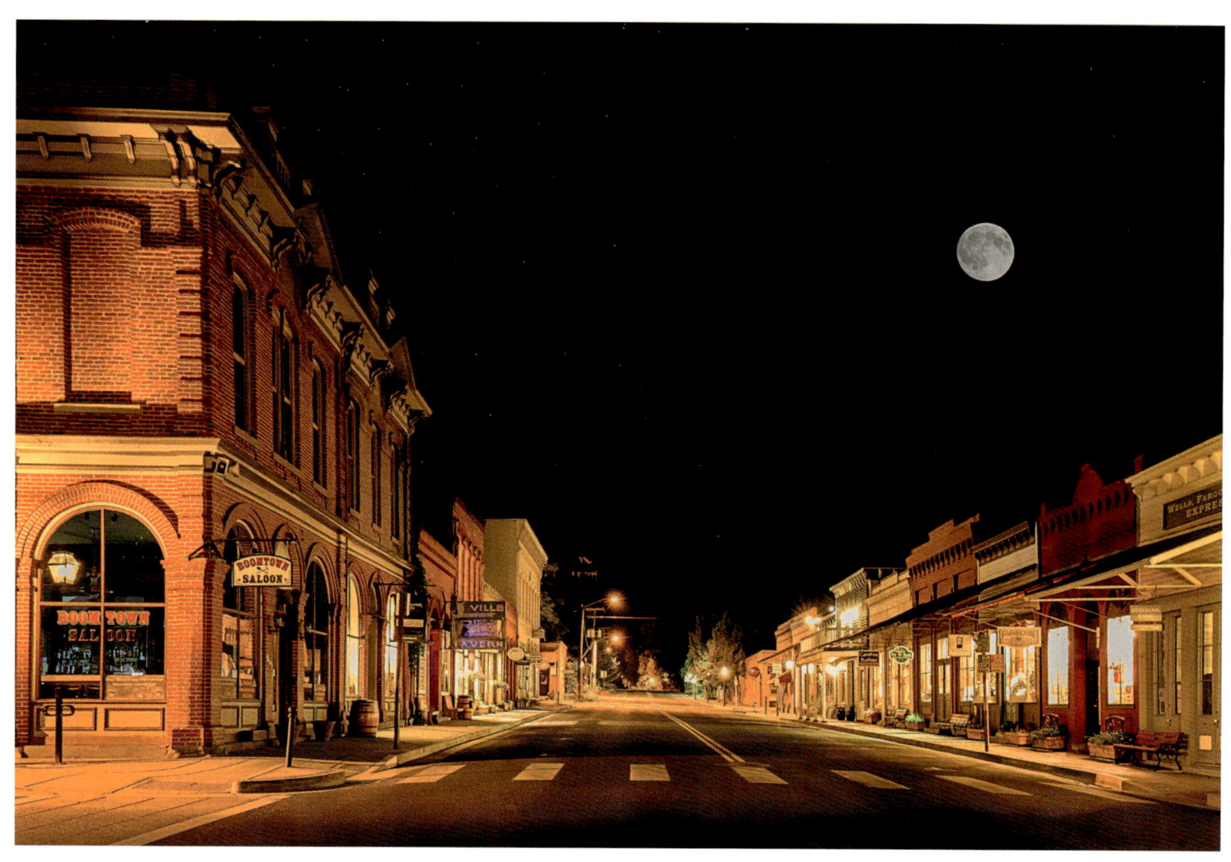

 Historic Jacksonville's city center. *Photo by Gary Hill.*

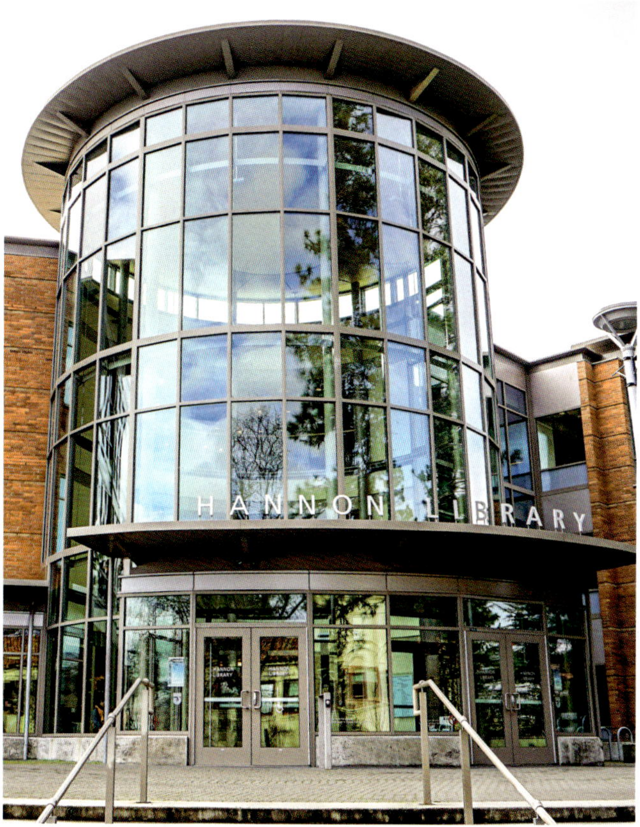

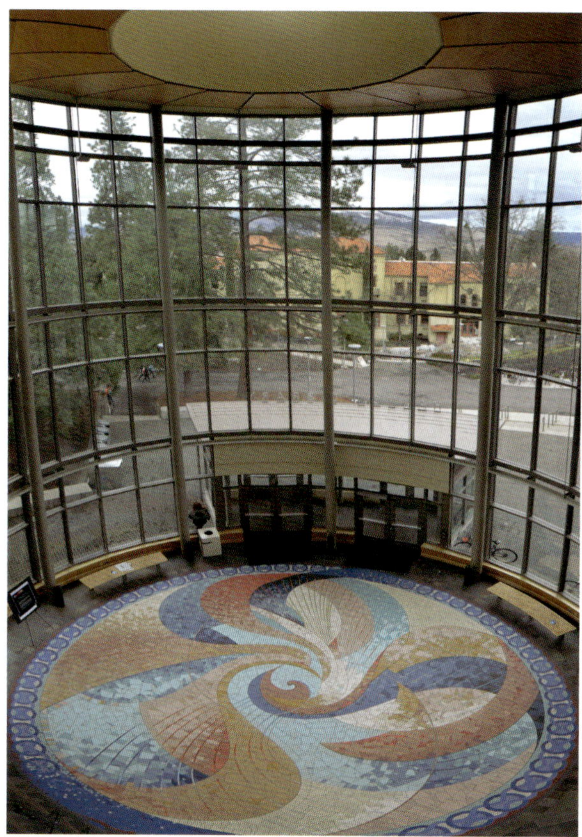

Hannon Library, Southern Oregon University, Ashland. *Photo by Atana Morell.* • Hannon Library rotunda, Southern Oregon University, Ashland. *Resonance & Dispersion* mosaic by Robert Stout and Stephanie Jurs. *Photo by Barbara Tricarico.*

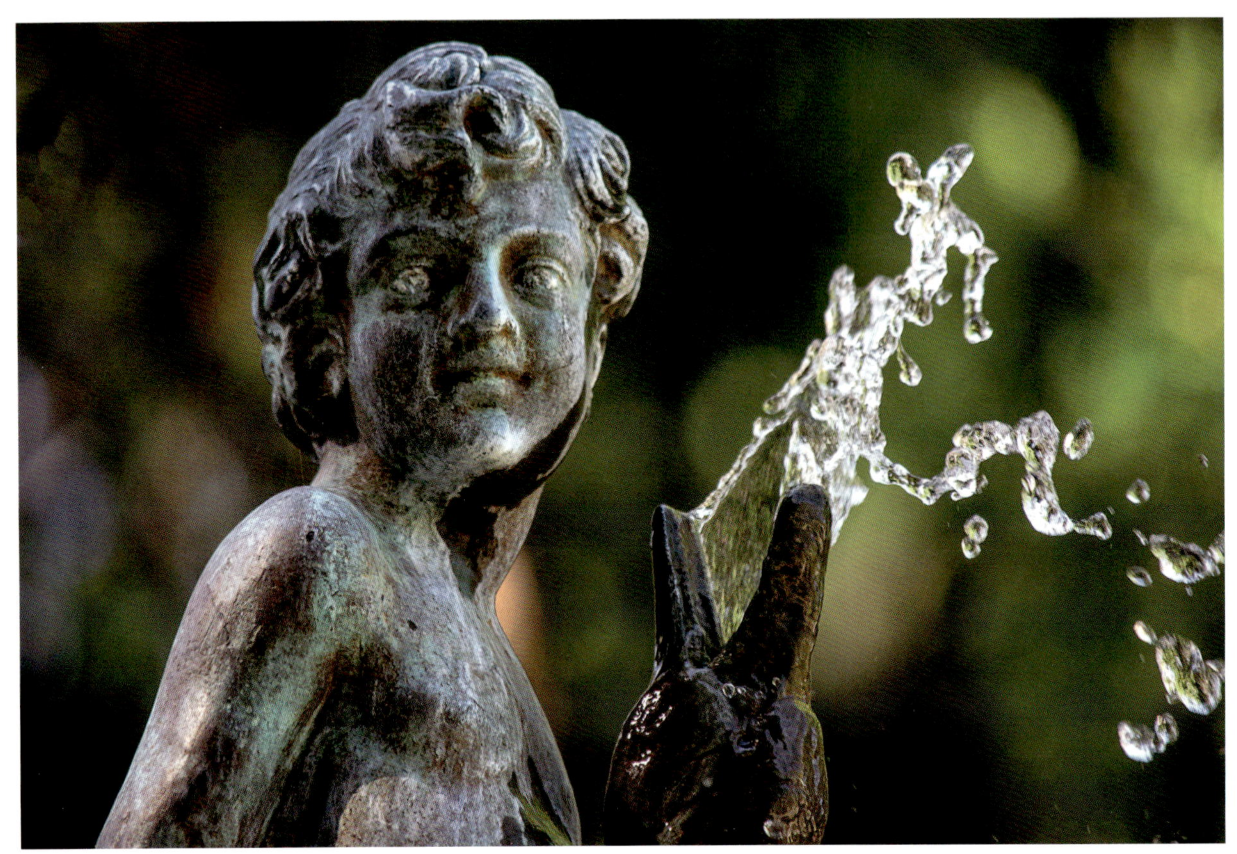

 Lithia Park's Butler-Perozzi Fountain in Lithia Park, Ashland, was installed in 1916. *Photo by David Lorenz Winston.*

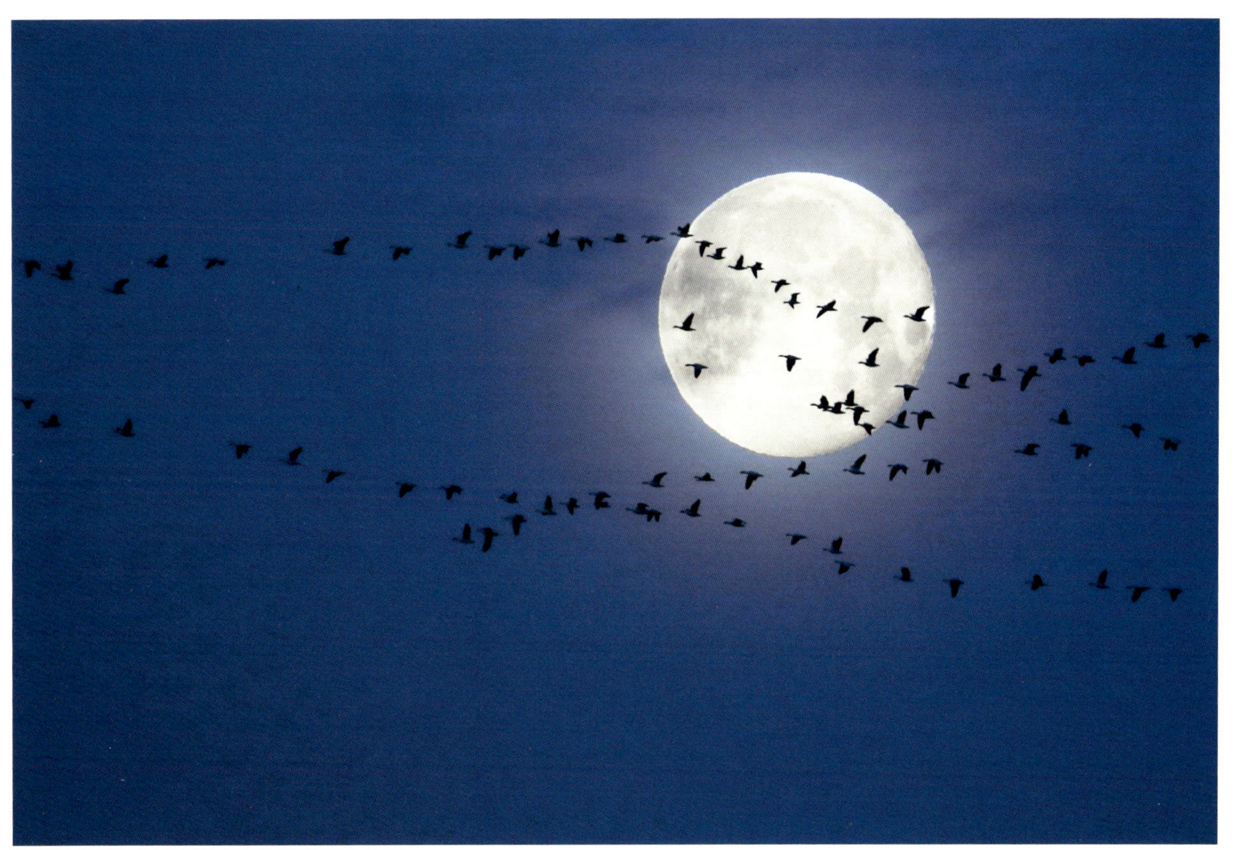

Snow geese and moon. *Photo by Dan Elster.*

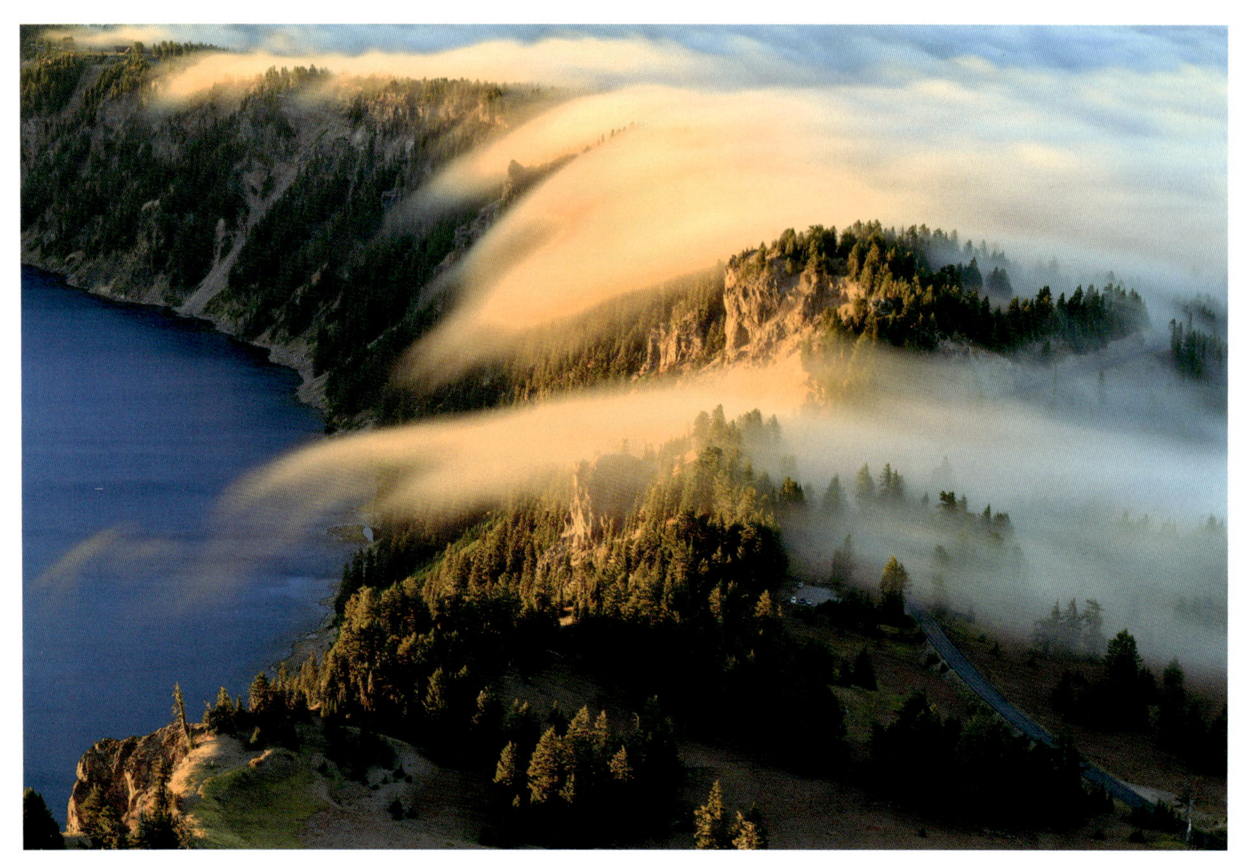

Crater Lake. *Photo by Vldn Taylor.*

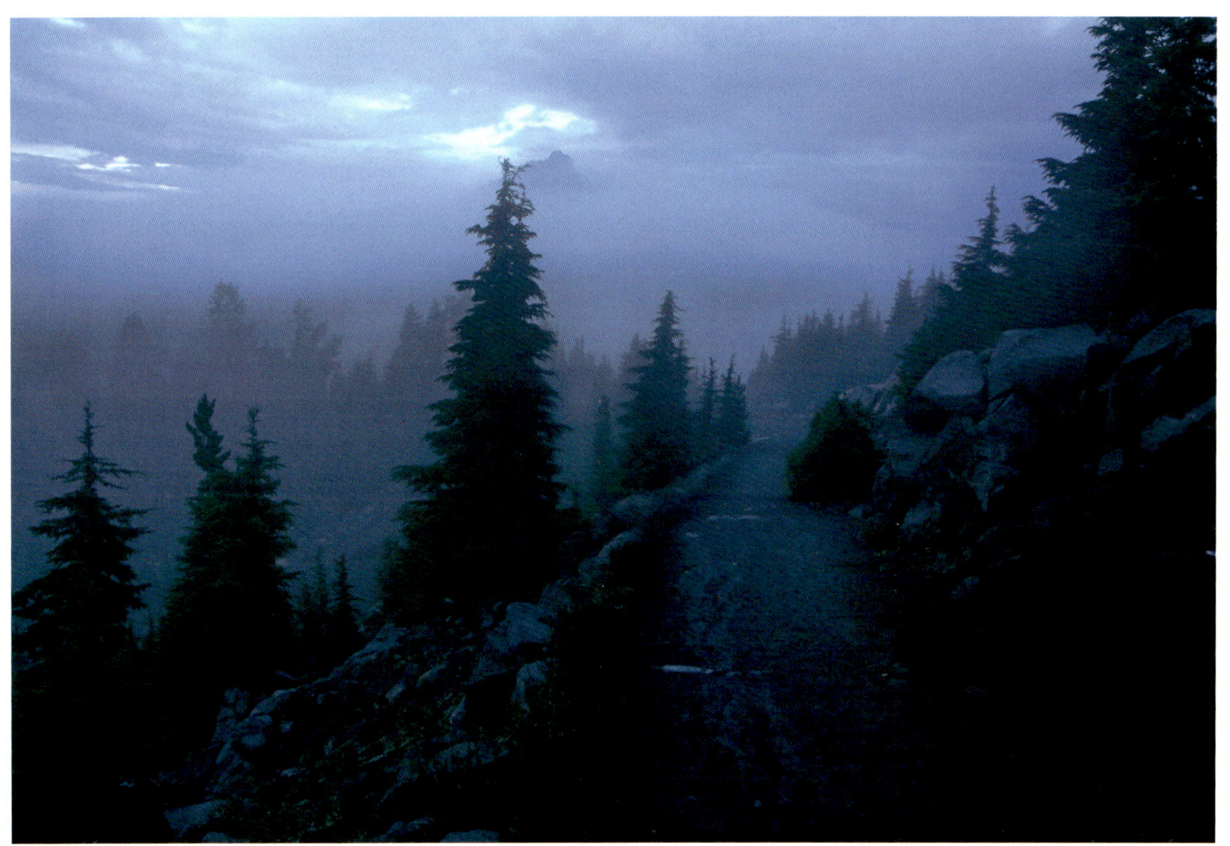

Watchman Trail, Crater Lake. *Photo by Jay Newman.*

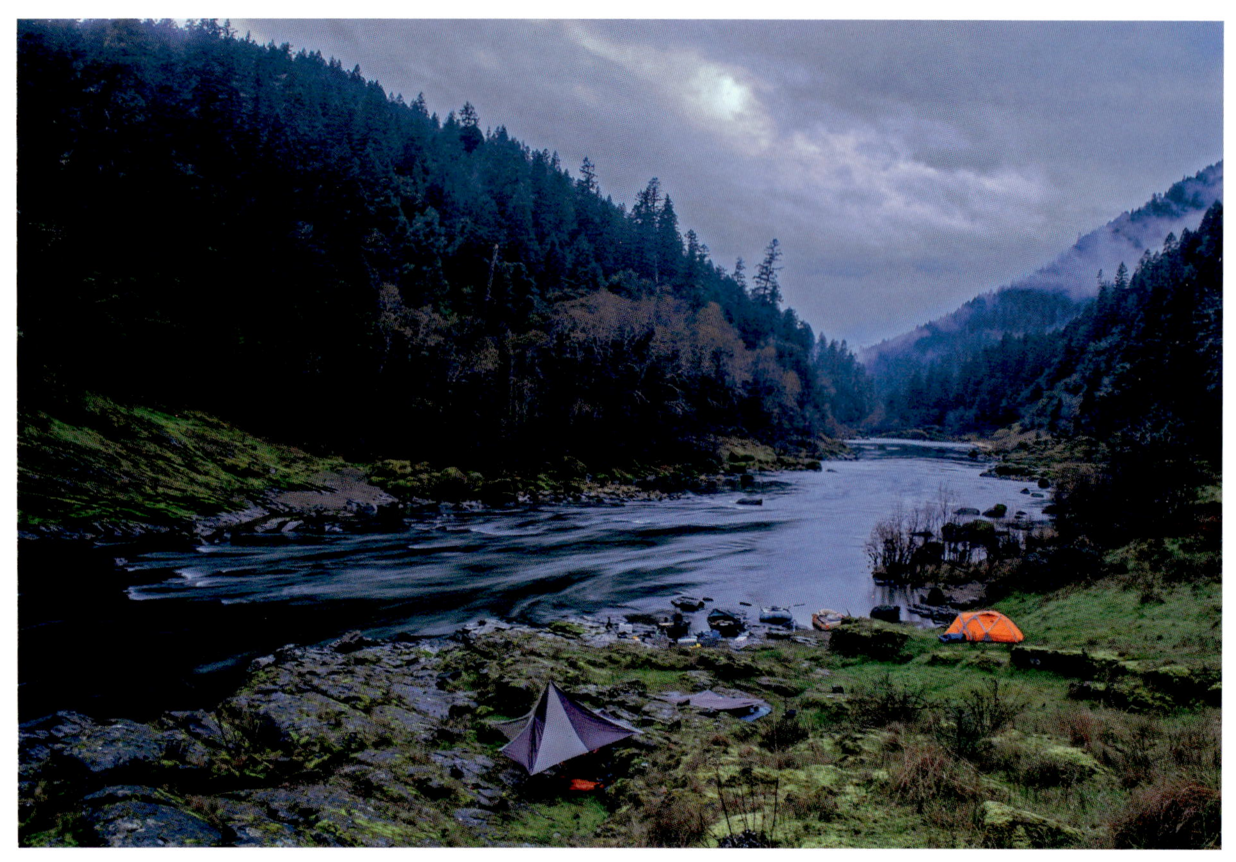

 Camping along the Rogue River at Tacoma. *Photo by Will Volpert, Indigo Creek Outfitters.*

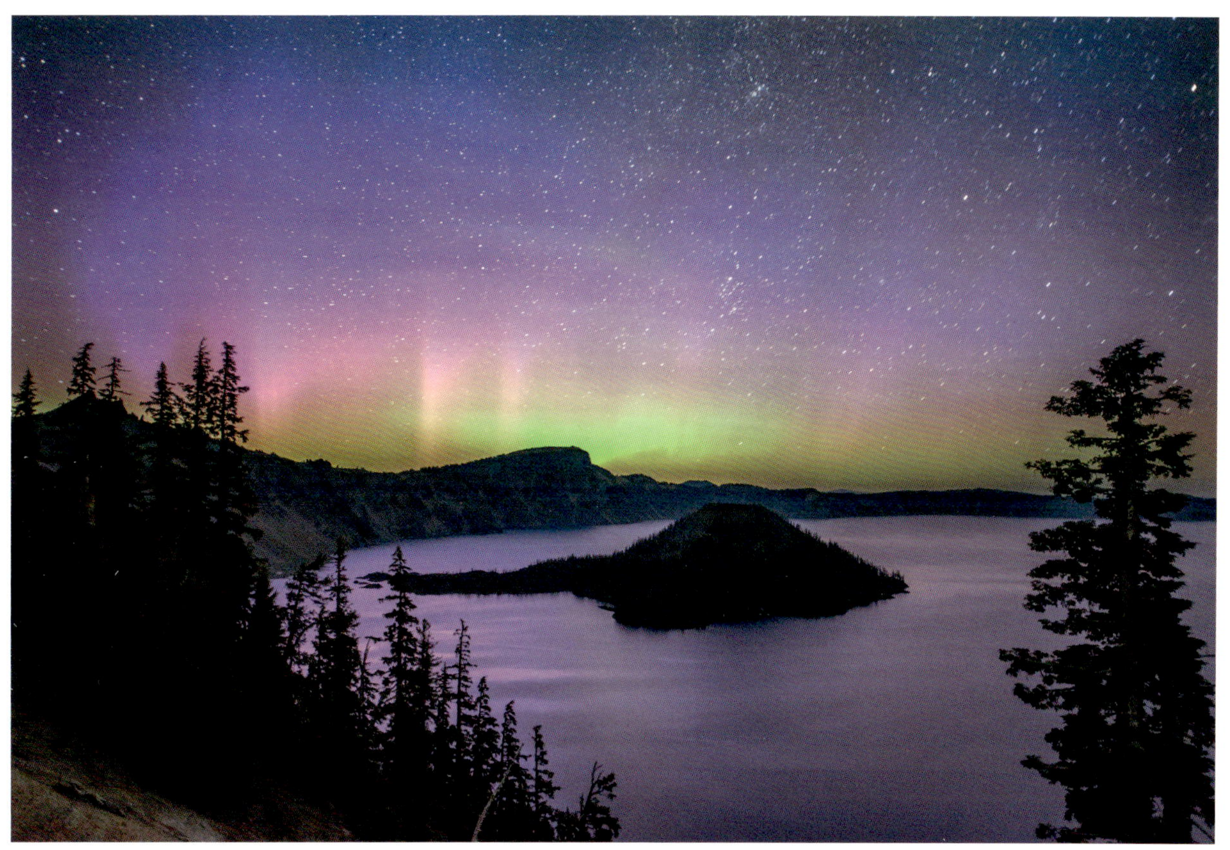

Aurora borealis over Wizard Island at Crater Lake. *Photo by Earshel Hogan.*

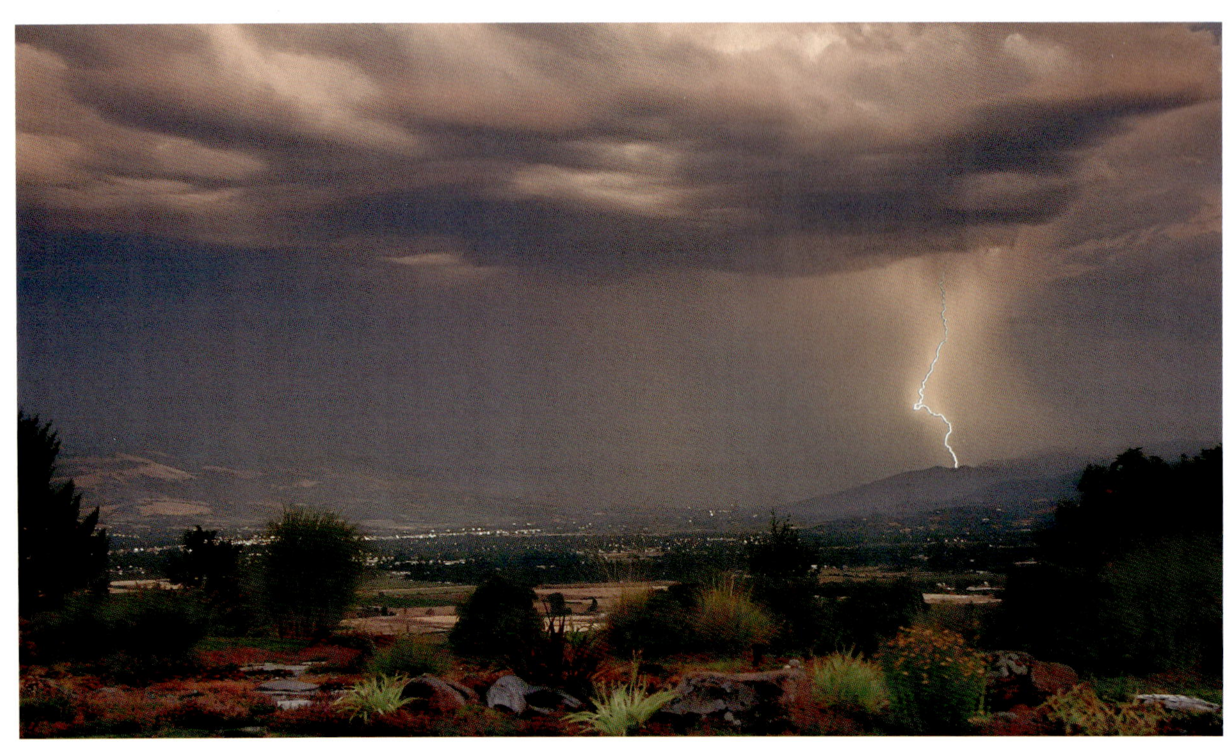

 Lightning over the Rogue Valley. *Photo by Gary Hill.*

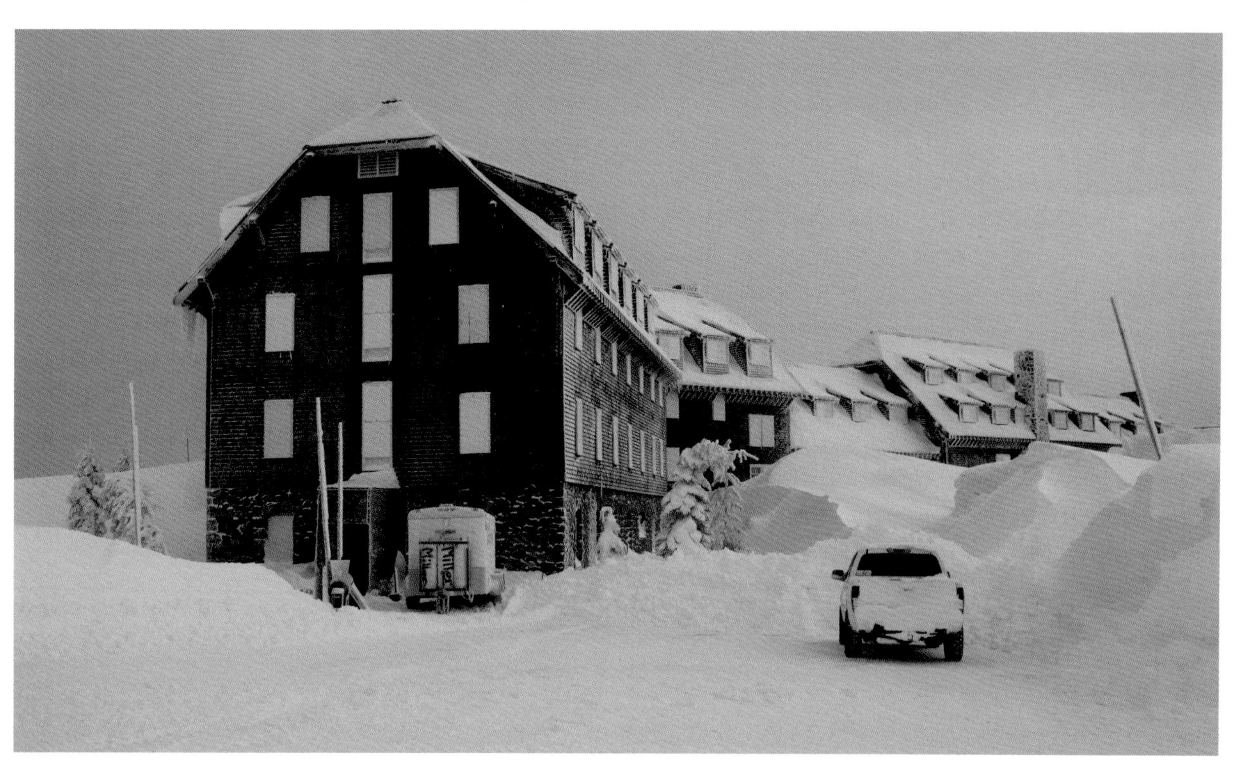

Crater Lake Lodge. *Photo by John Kirk.*

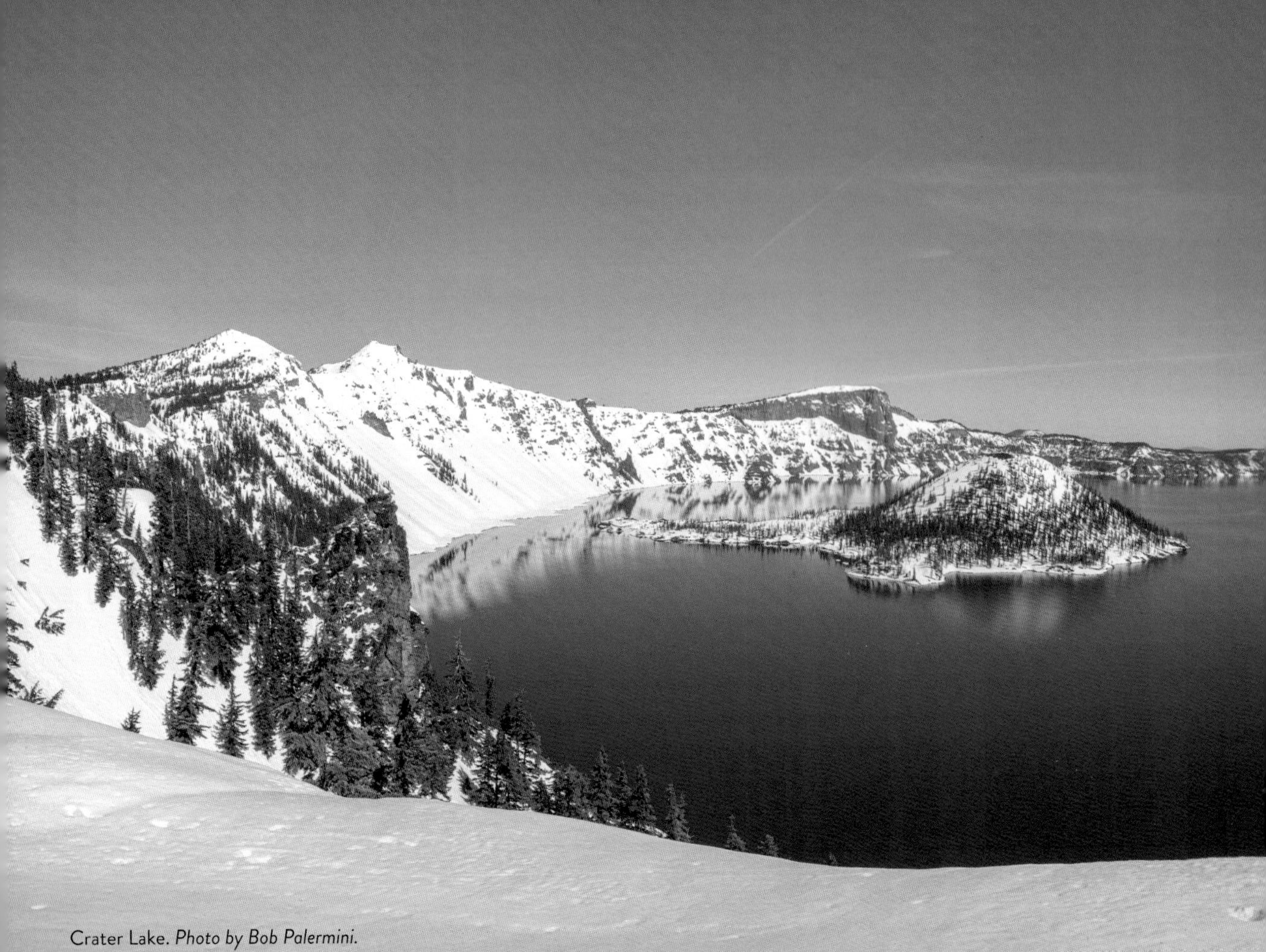

Crater Lake. *Photo by Bob Palermini.*

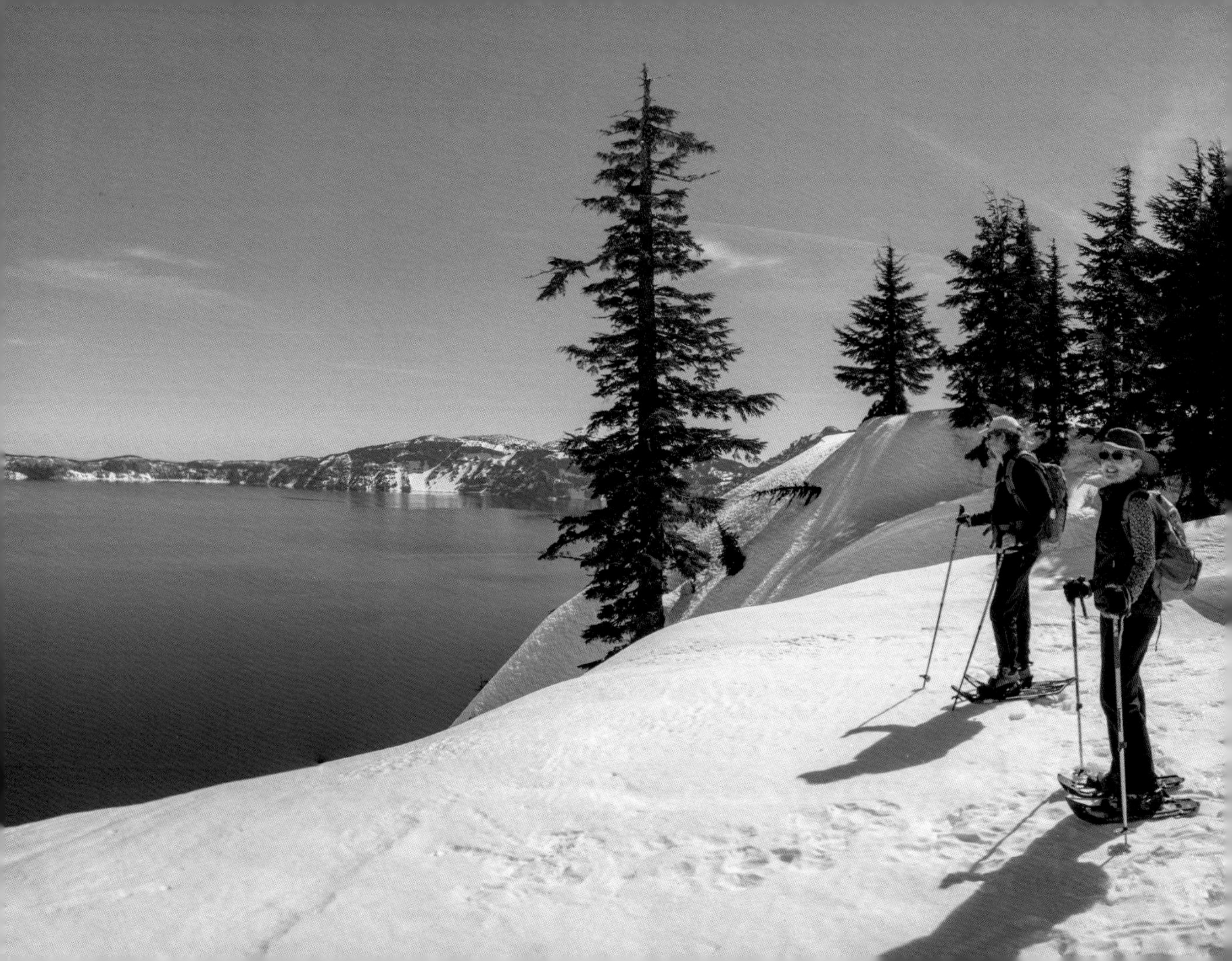

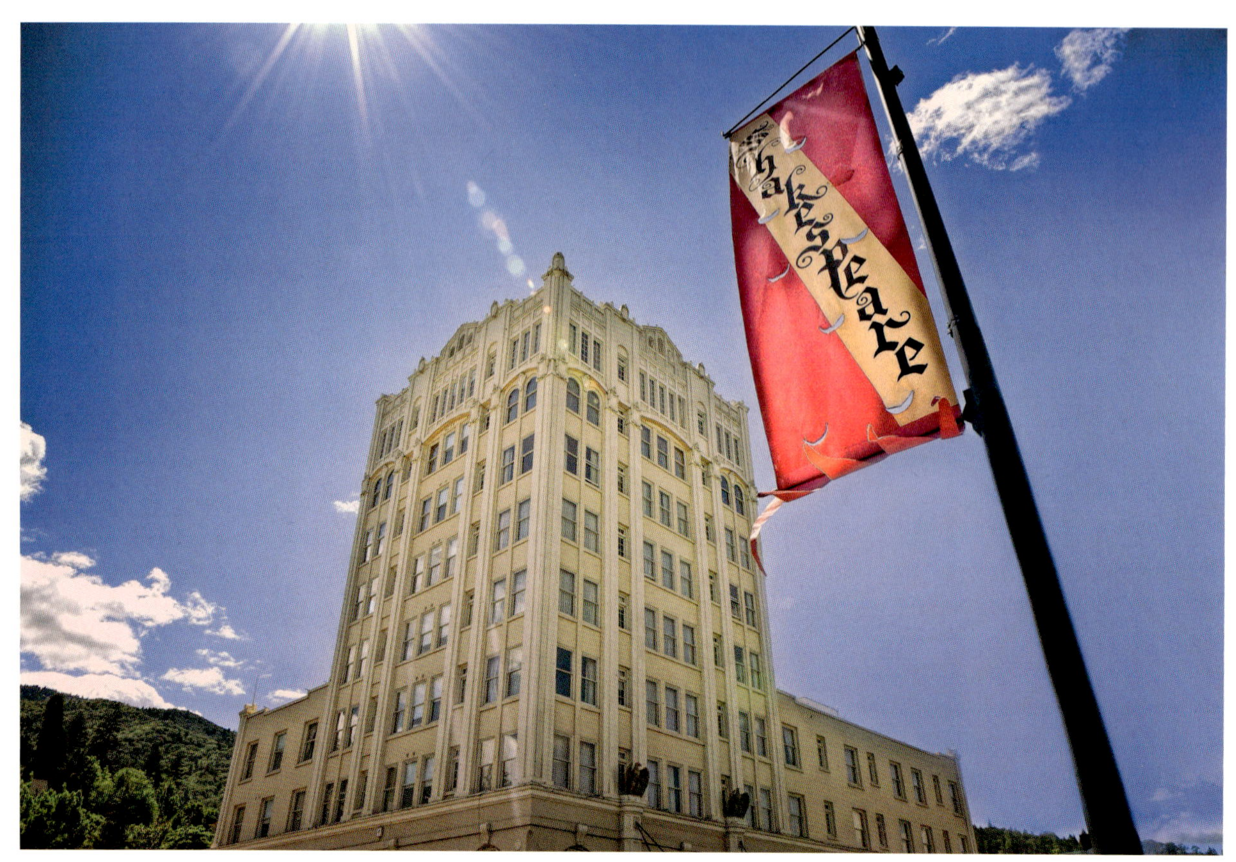

 Ashland Springs Hotel, built in 1925. *Photo by Barbara Tricarico.*

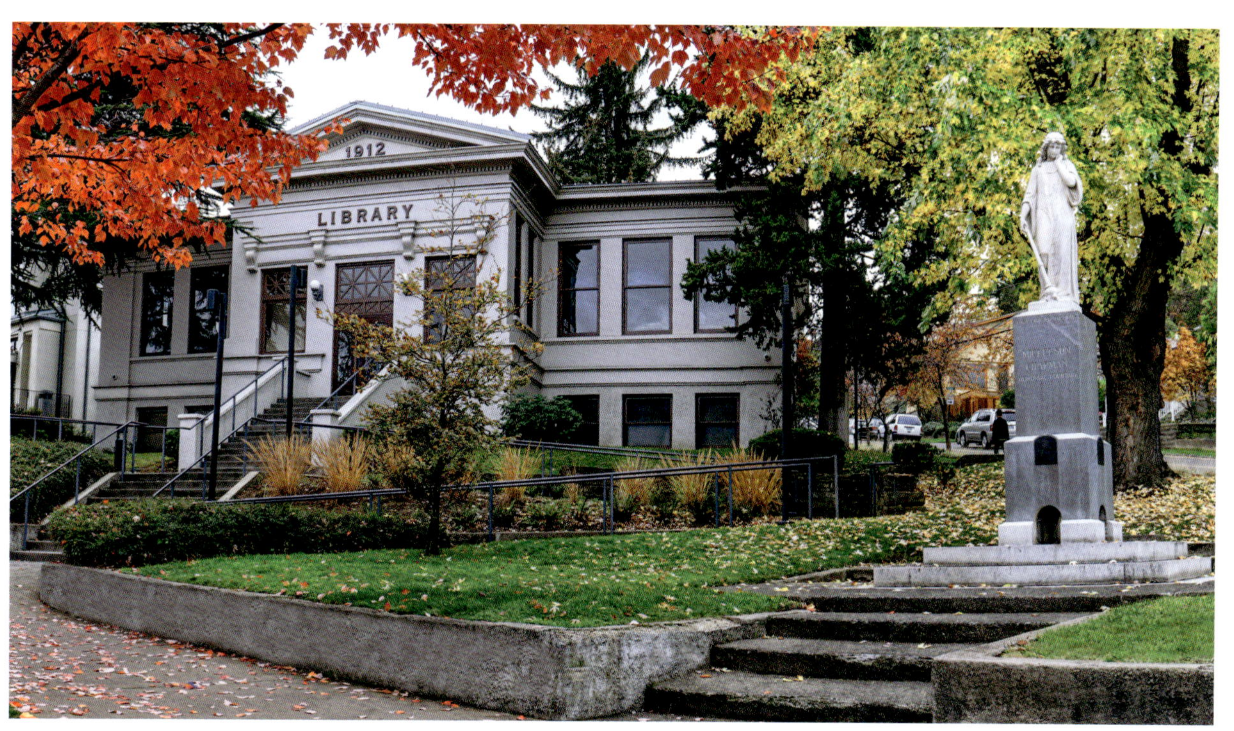

Ashland Library, built with a grant from Andrew Carnegie. Dedicated in 1912. *Photo by Cornelius Matteo.*

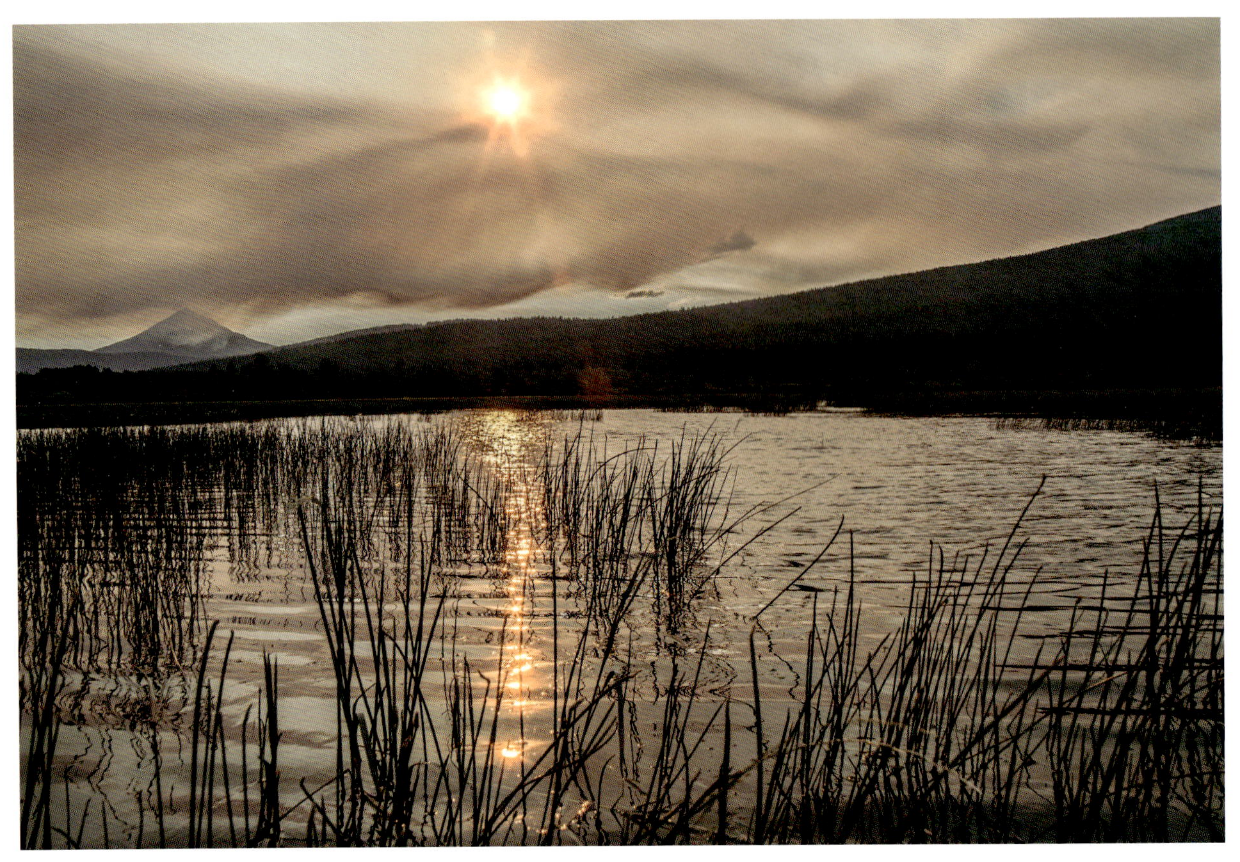

 Rocky Point, Upper Klamath Lake. *Photo by Diana Standing.*

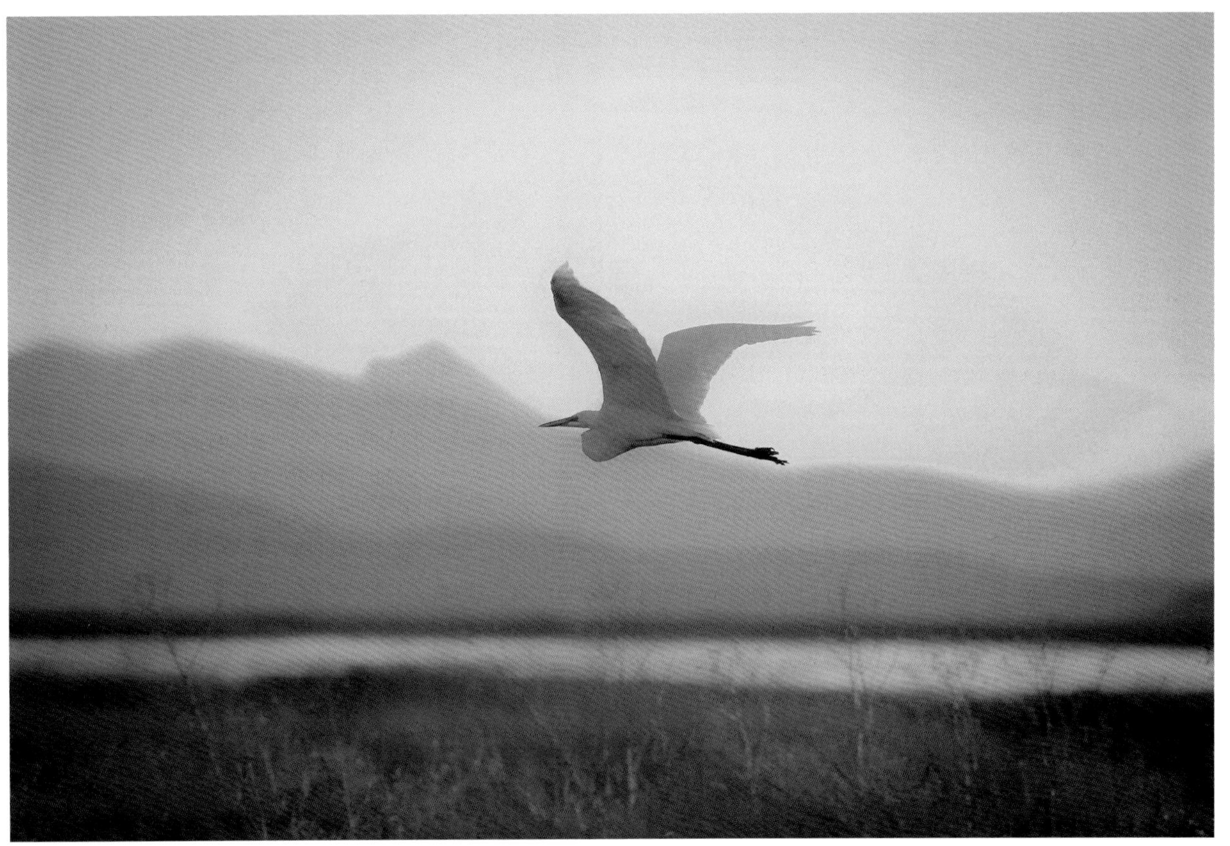

Great egret at Klamath National Wildlife Refuge. *Photo by Terry Fisher.*

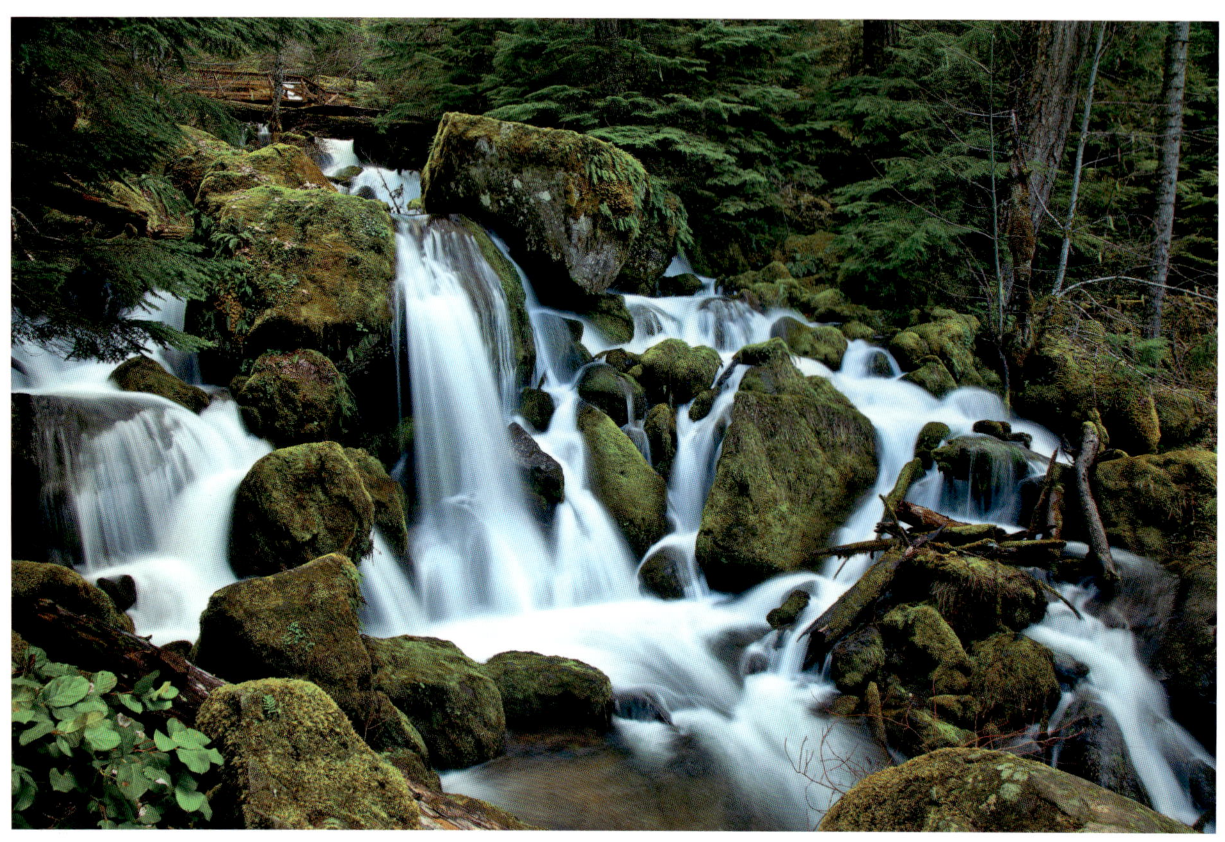

 Lower Watson Falls, Umpqua National Forest. *Photo by John Christer Petersen.*

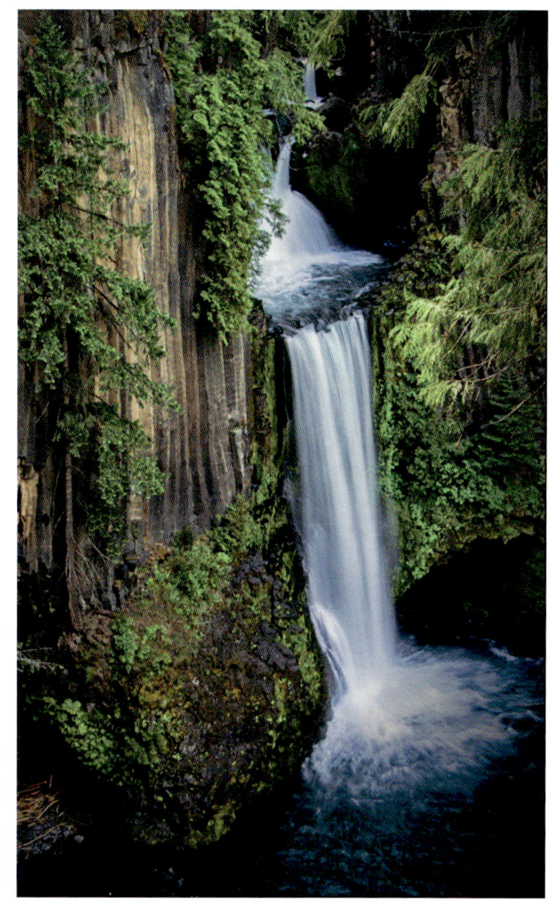

Toketee Falls. *Photo by Alana Lynn Starkweather.*

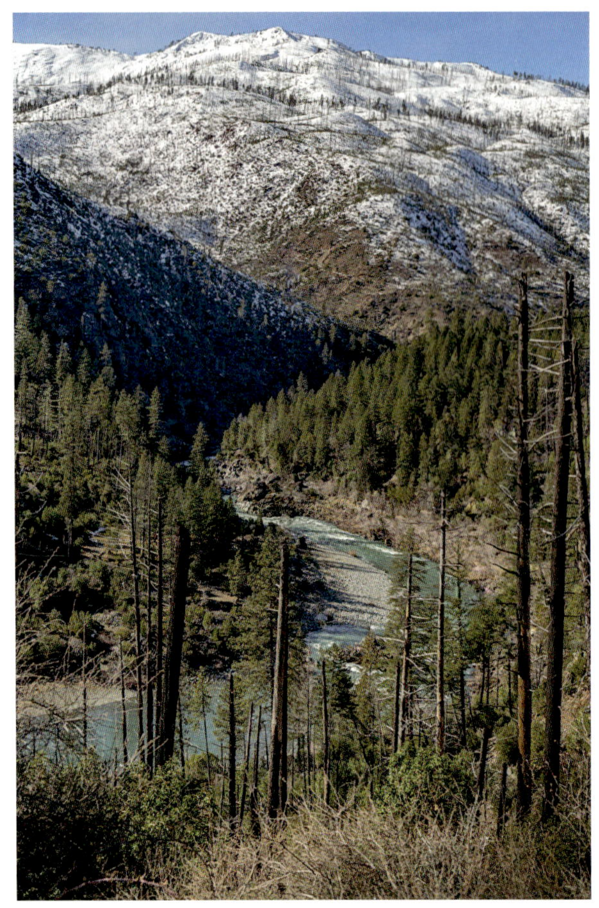

 Illinois River. *Photo by Alana Lynn Starkweather.*

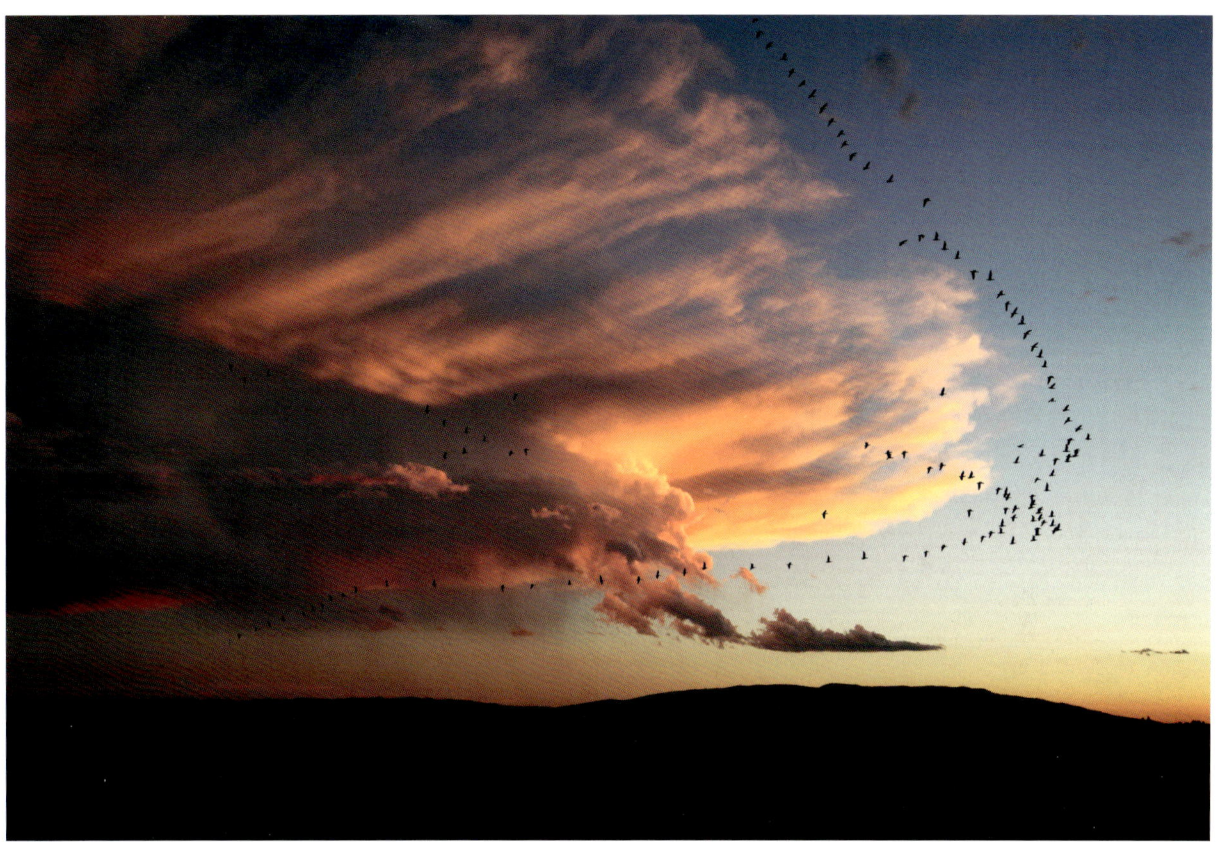

Birds at sunset. *Photo by John Kirk.* • (Page 54) Caveman Bridge and Taprock Northwest Grill, Grants Pass. *Photo by Earshel Hogan.*

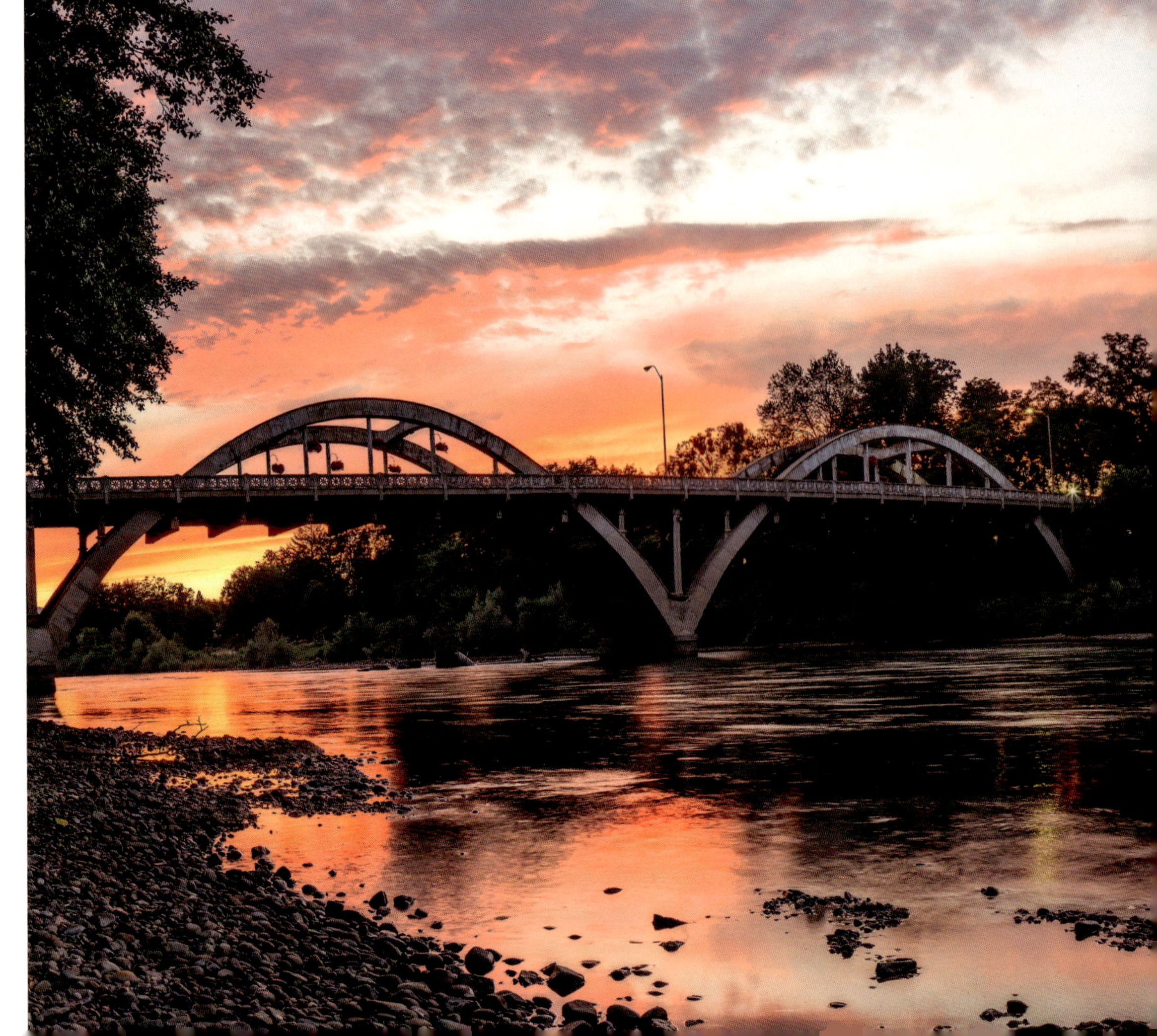

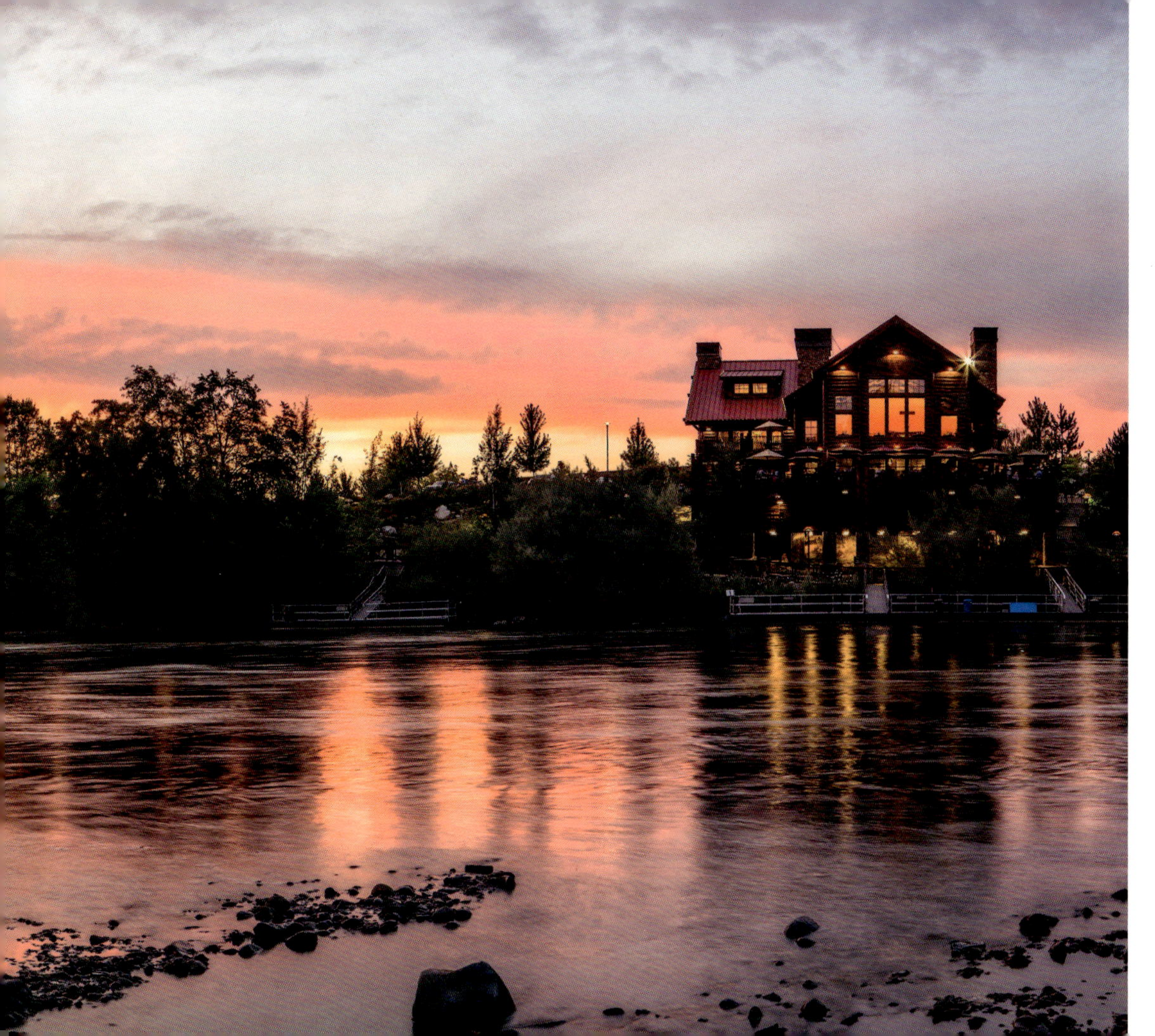

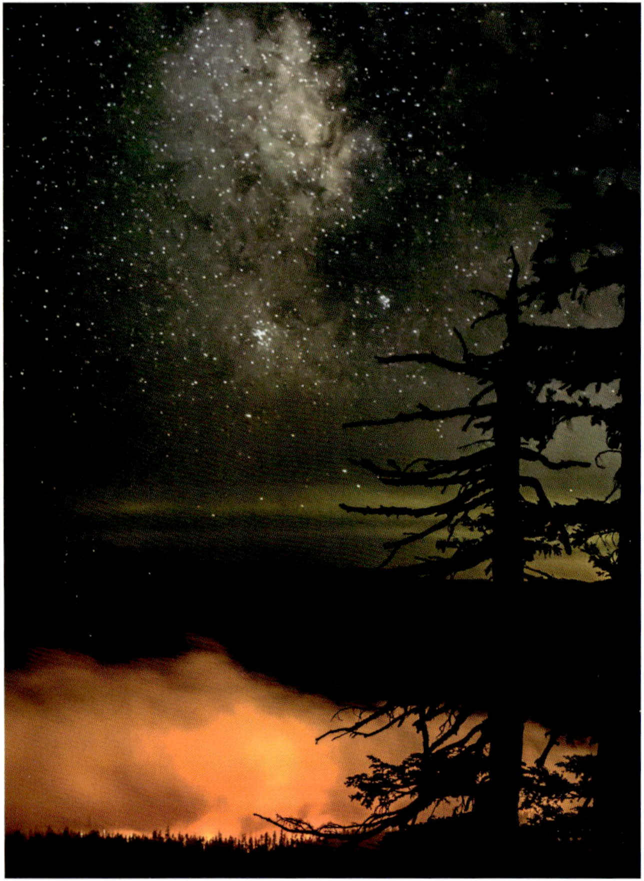

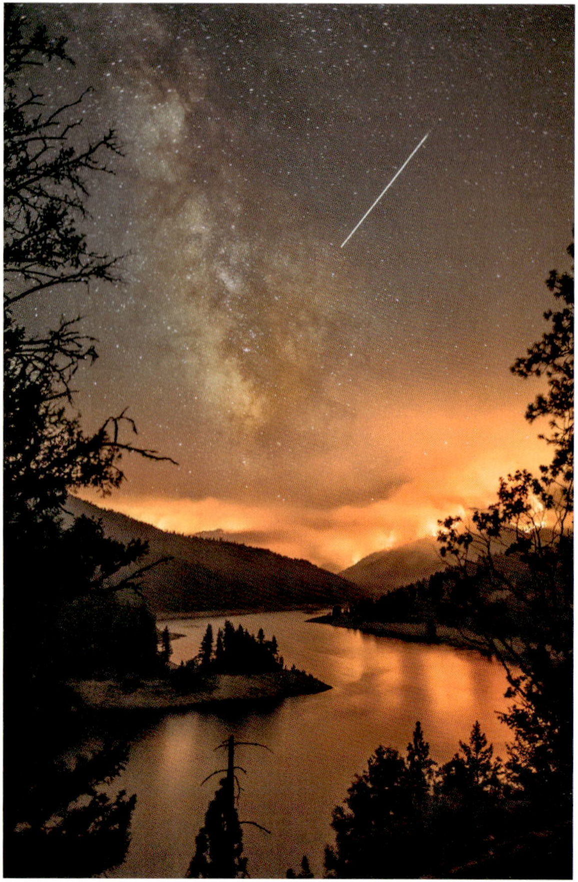

 Milky Way and fire at Crater Lake. *Photo by Vivian McAleavey.* • Milky Way and fire at Applegate Lake. *Photo by Rudy Dierks.*

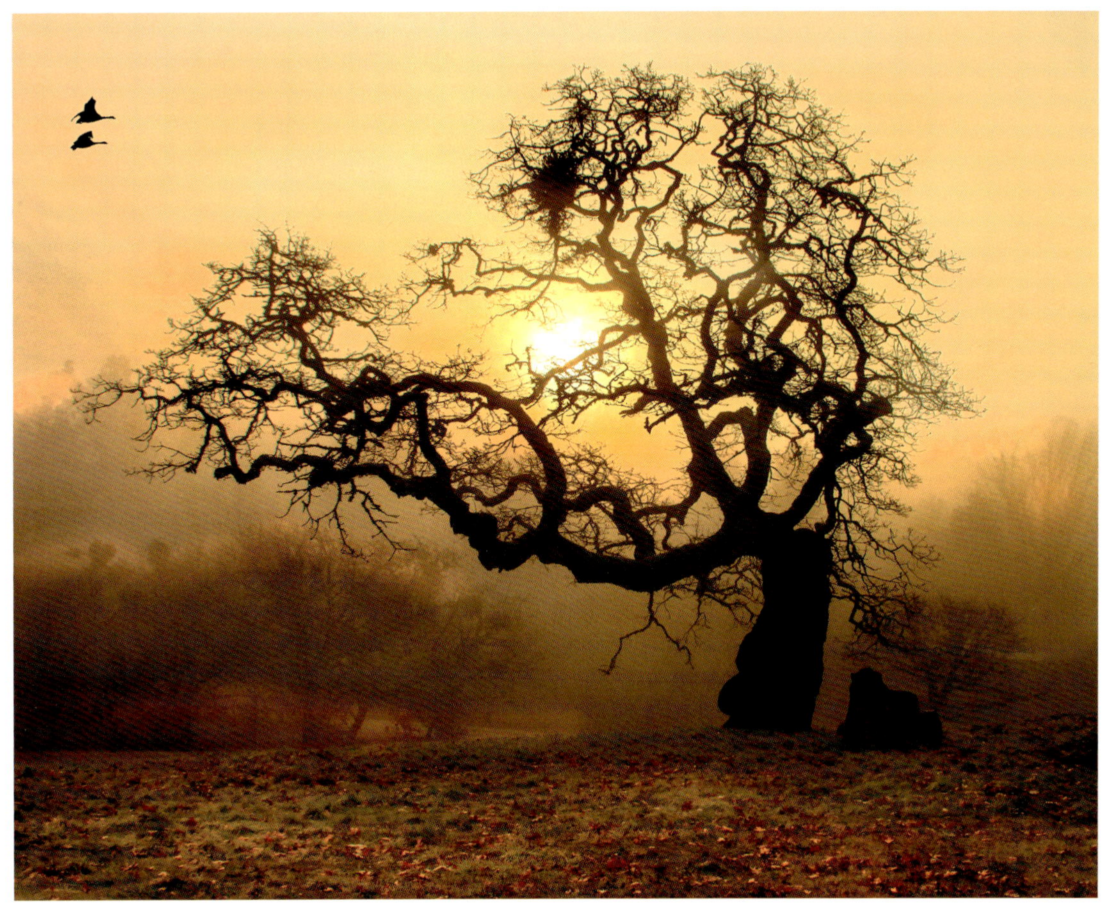

Tree in fog. *Photo by Neal R. Thompson.*

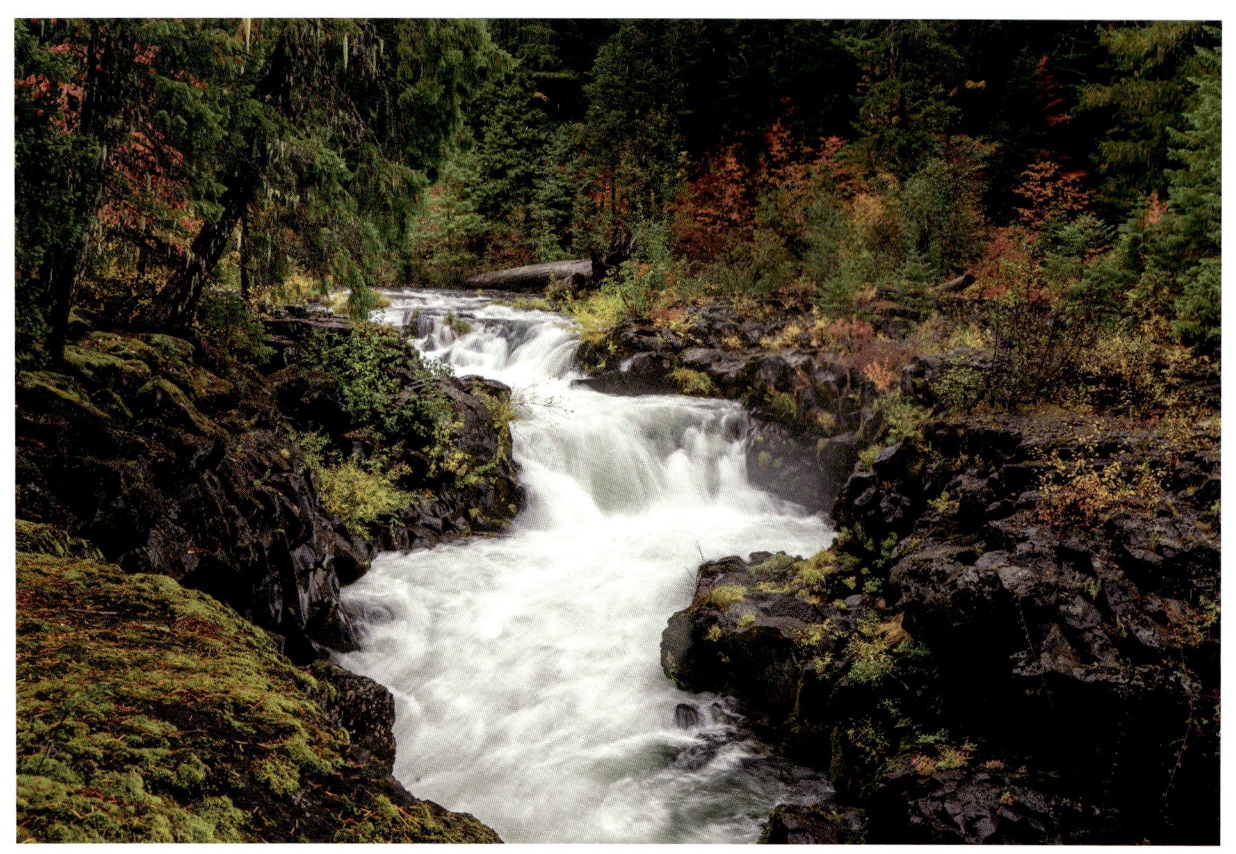

 Knob Falls, Upper Rogue Trail. *Photo by Bob Palermini.*

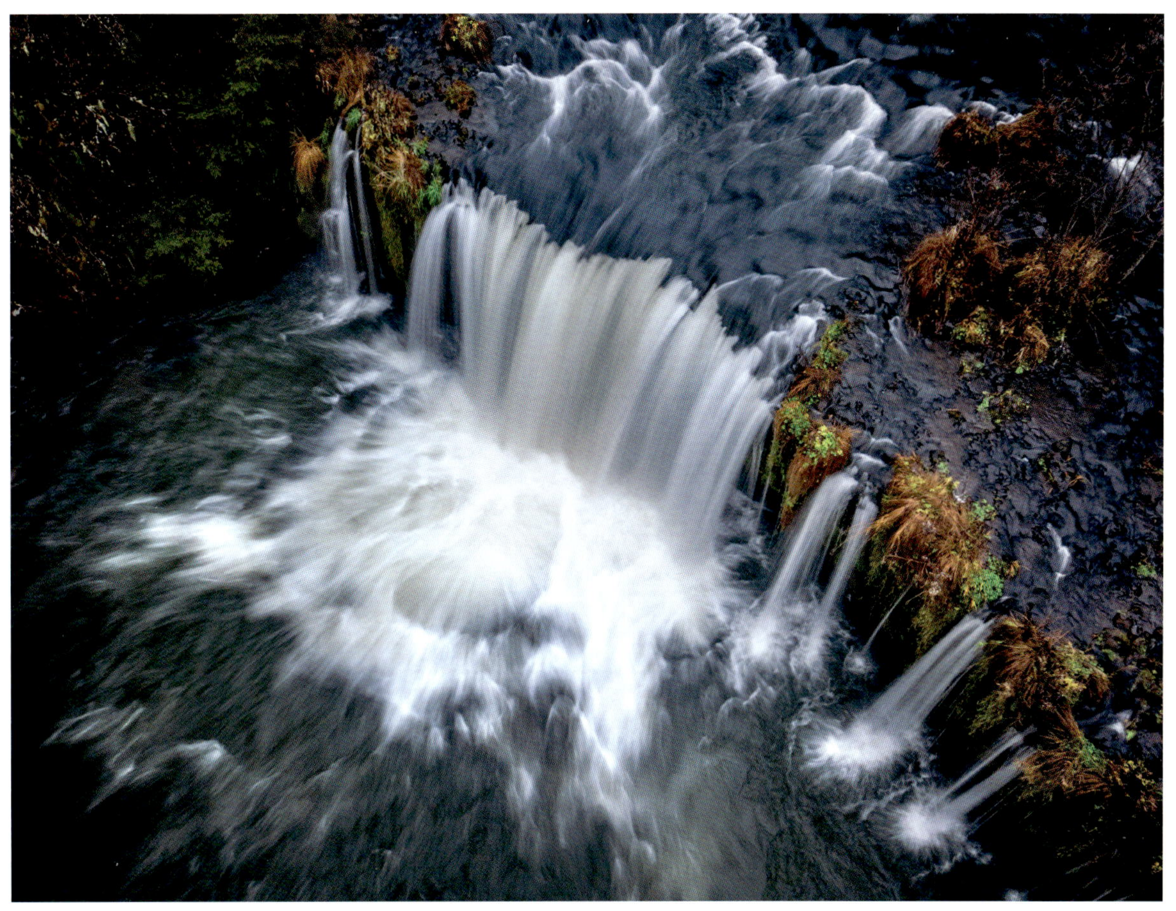

Butte Falls. *Photo by Brandon Herring.*

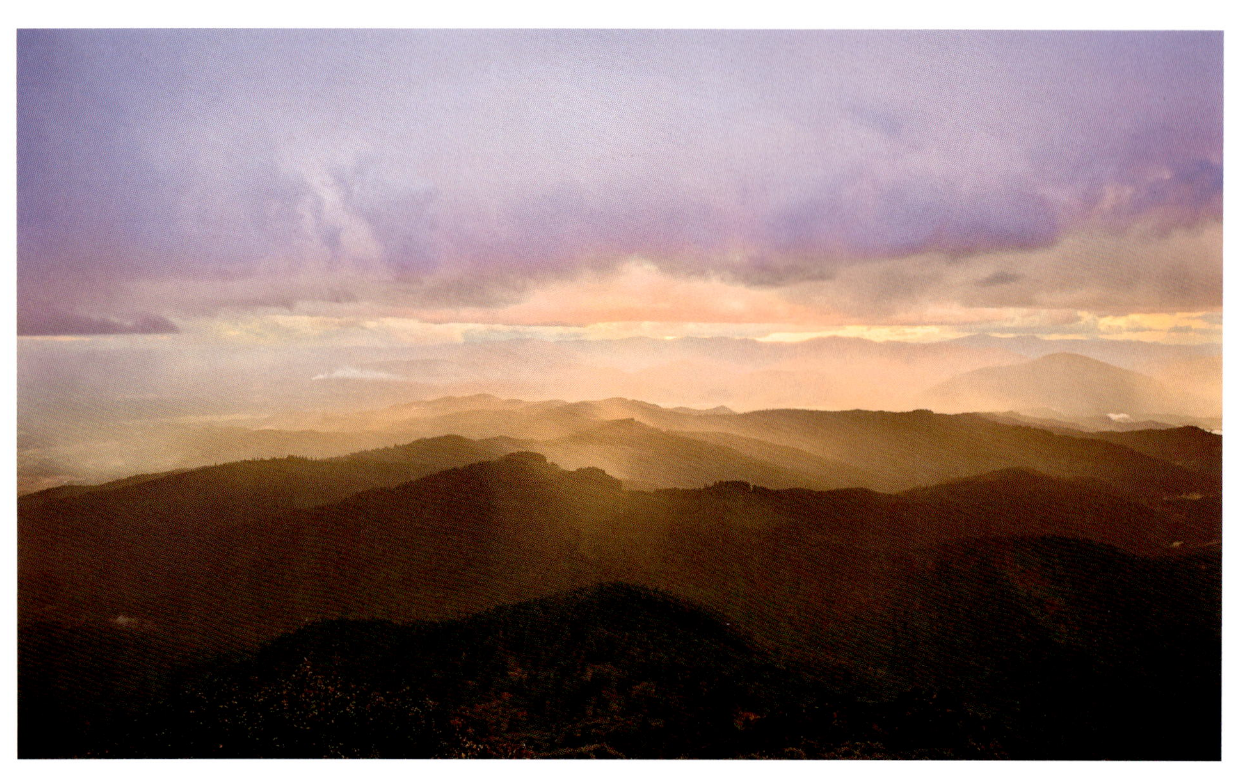

Selma storm. *Photo by Nomeca Hartwell.*

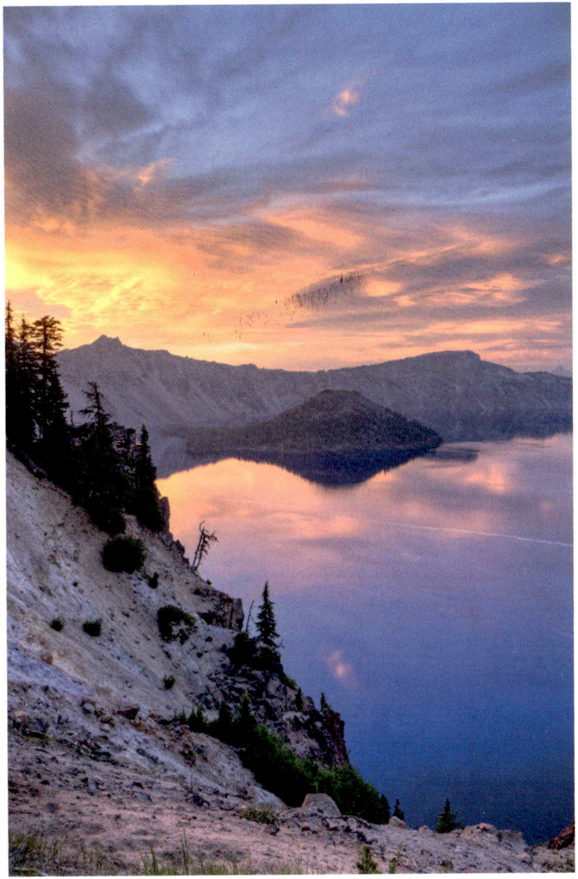

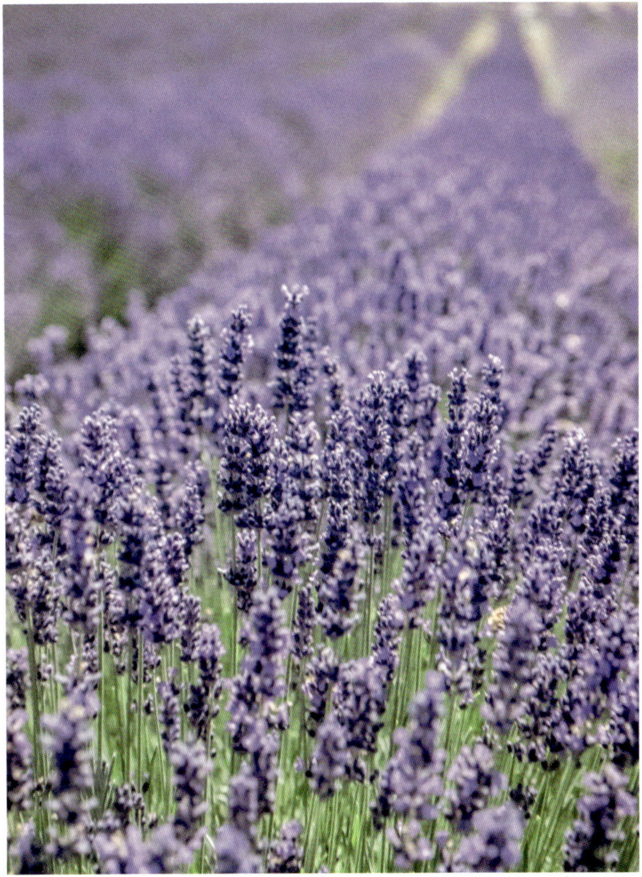

Crater Lake sunset. *Photo by Jay Newman.* • Lavender fields. *Photo by Vivian McAleavey.*

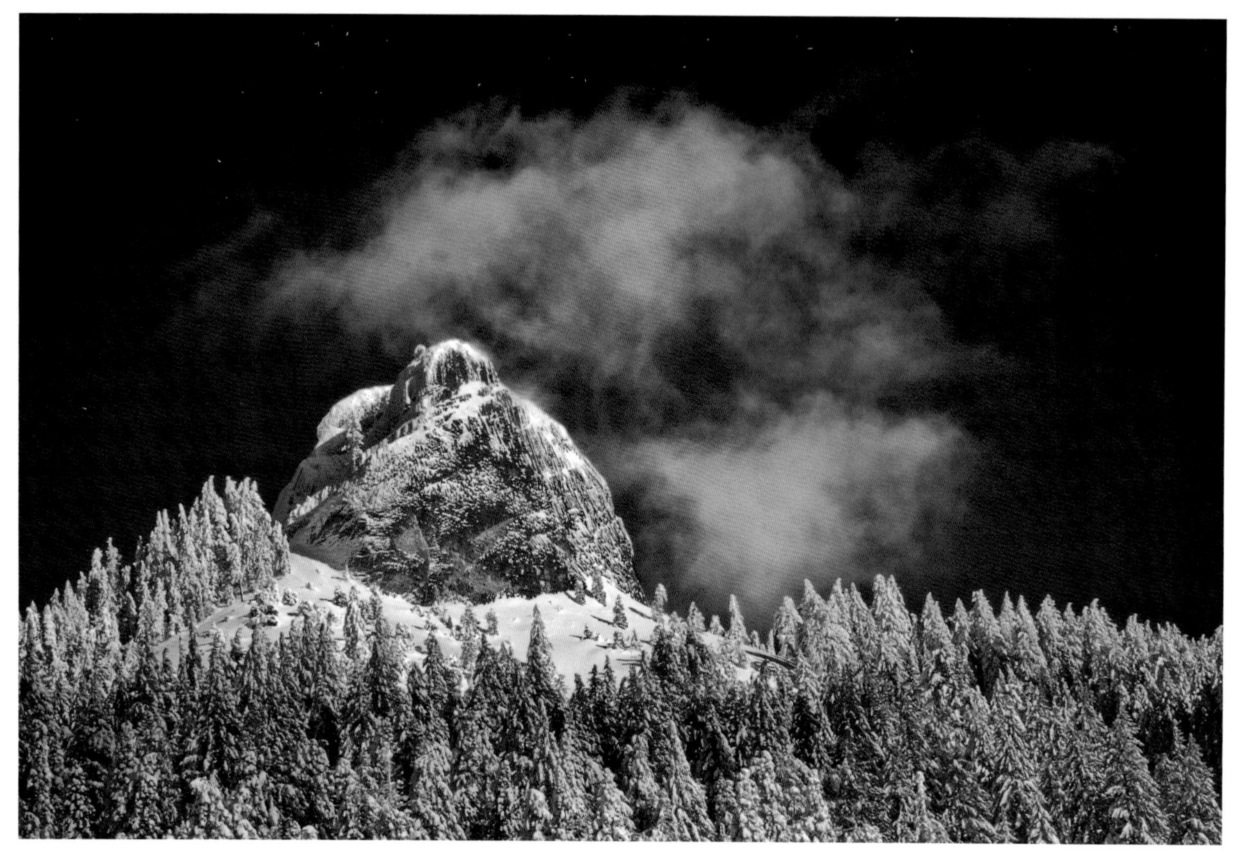

 Pilot Rock in the Cascade-Siskiyou National Monument. *Photo by Matt Witt.*

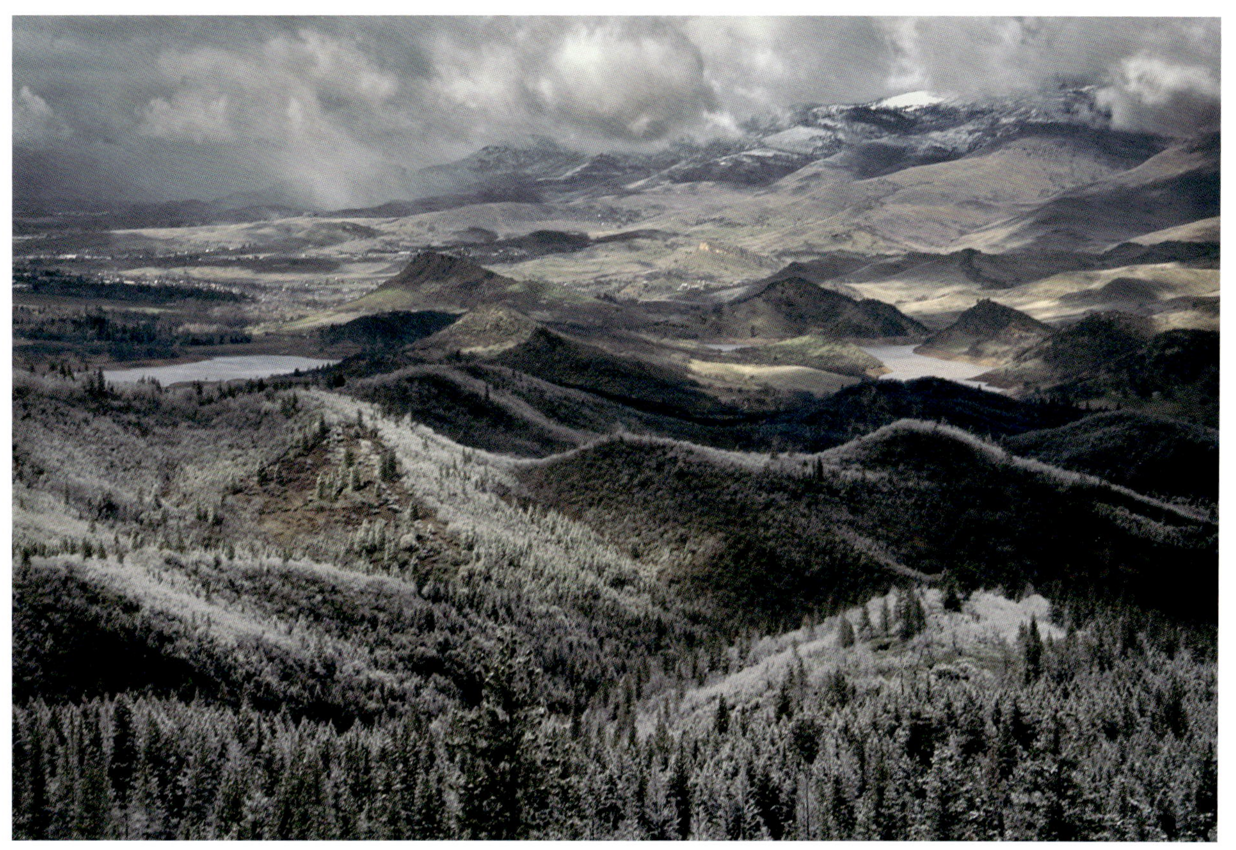

Emigrant Lake and Grizzly Peak. *Photo by Matt Witt.*

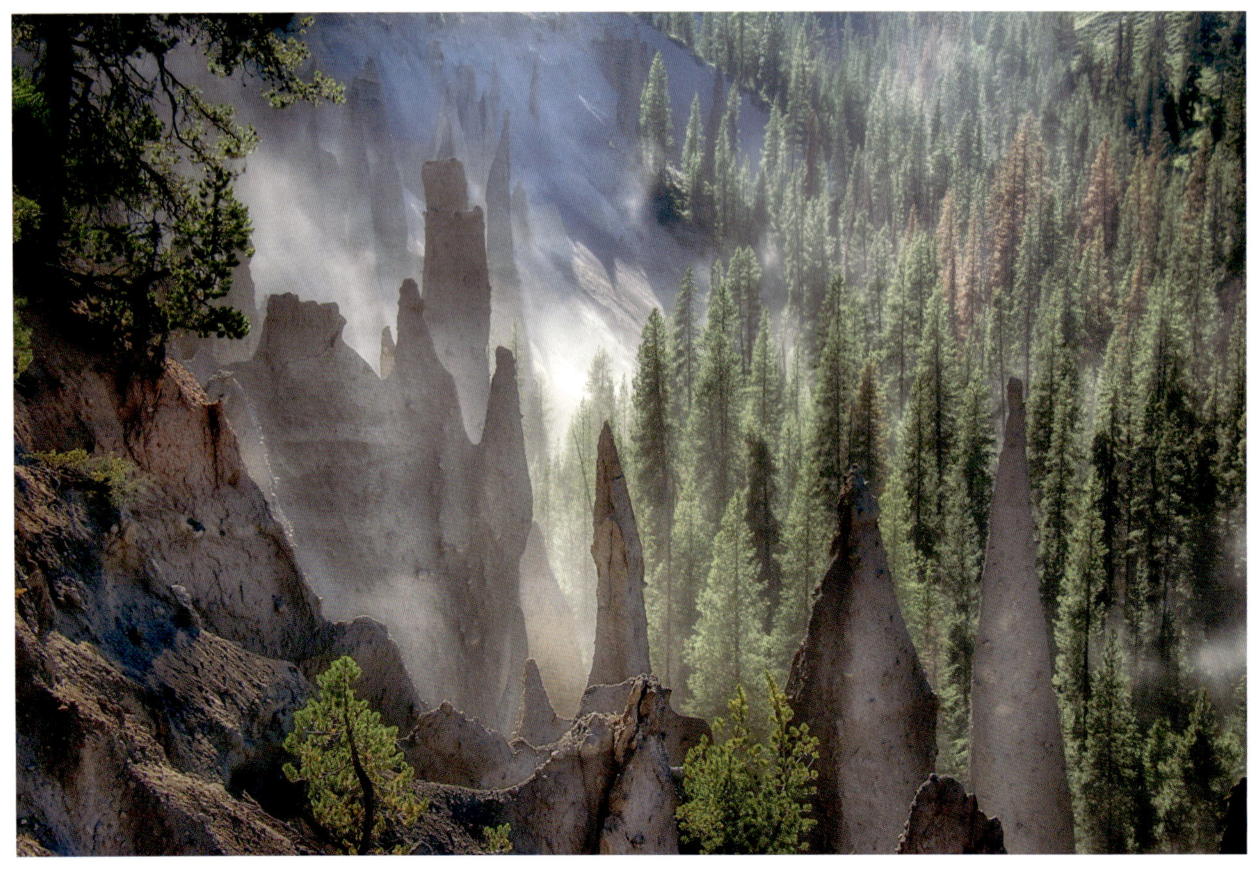

 The Pinnacles at Crater Lake National Park. *Photo by Barbara Tricarico.*

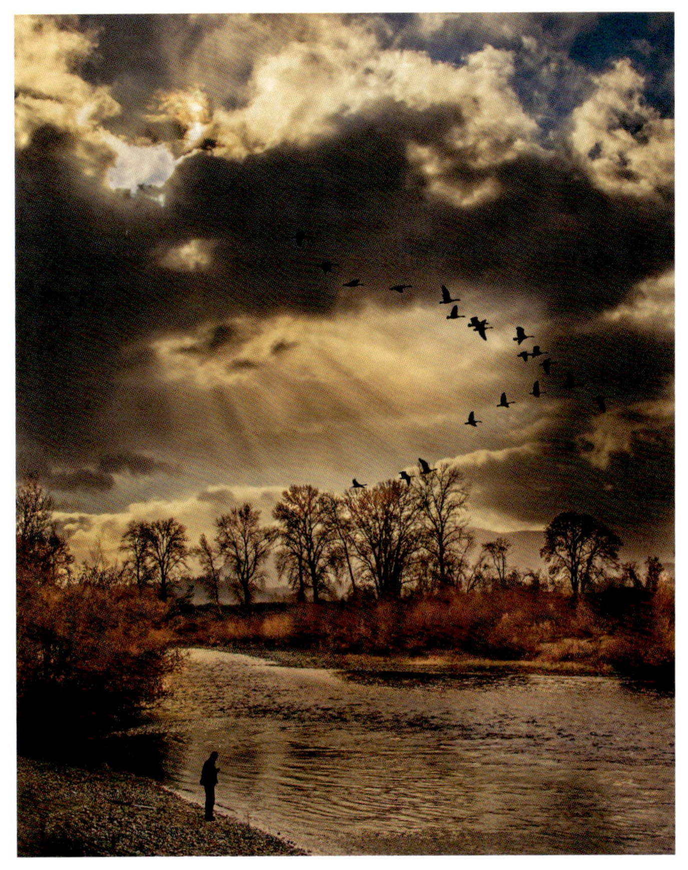

Rogue River, Grants Pass. *Photo by Neal R. Thompson.*

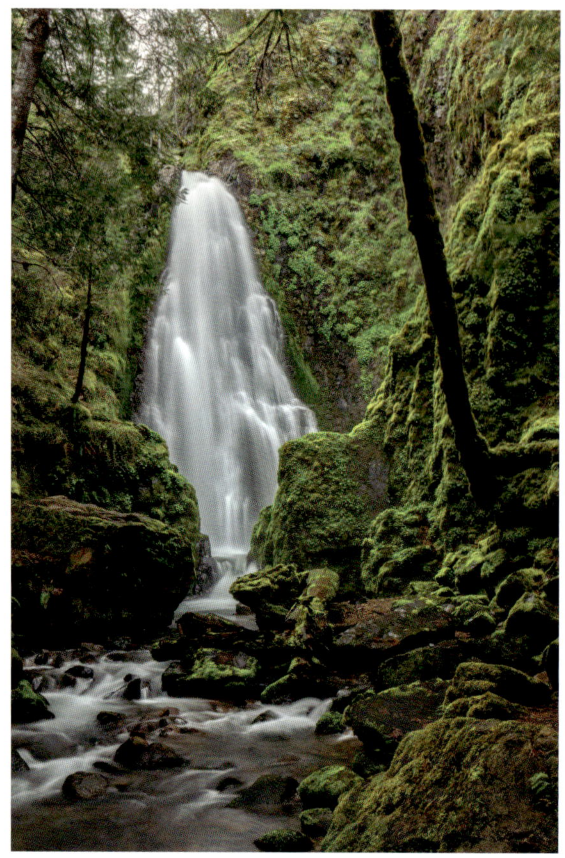

 Susan Creek Falls. *Photo by Sue Newman.*

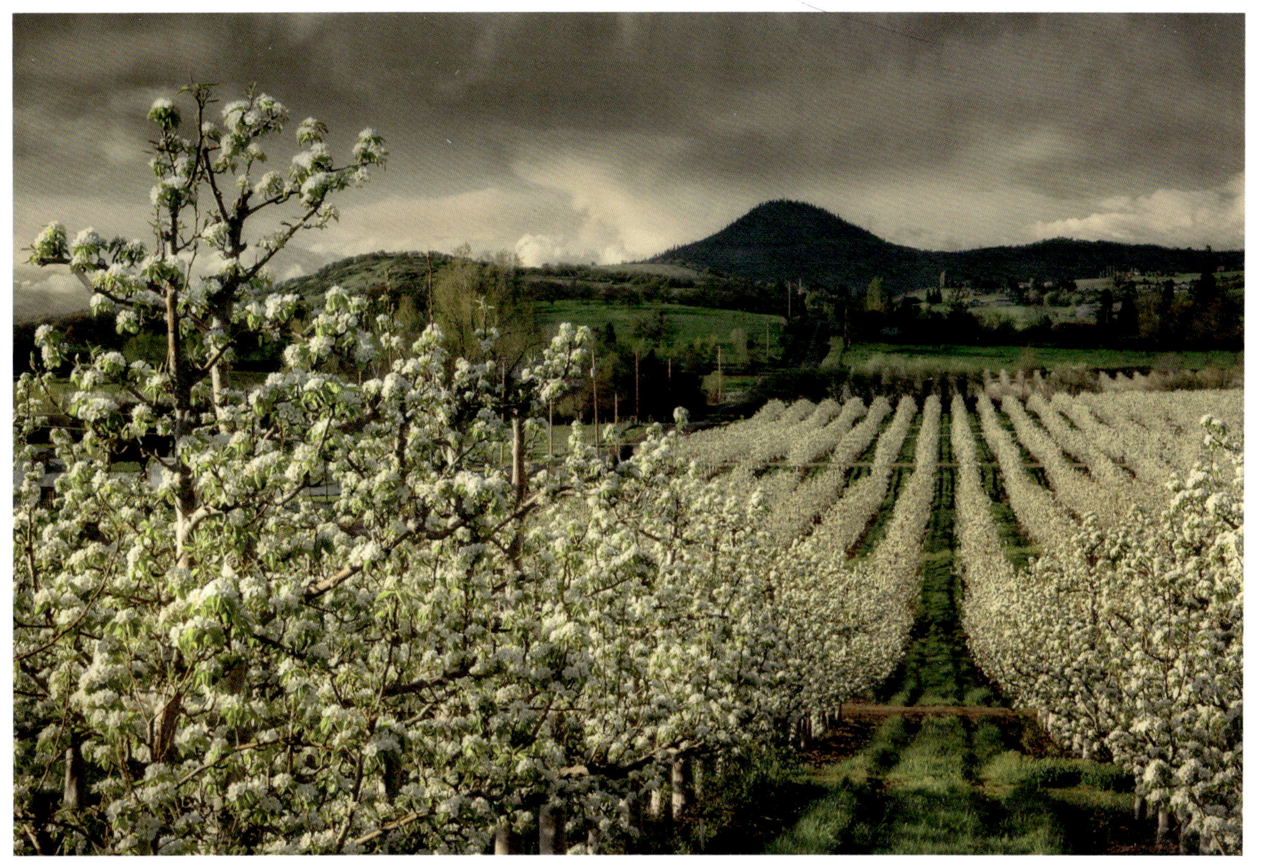

Pear trees. *Photo by David Lorenz Winston.*

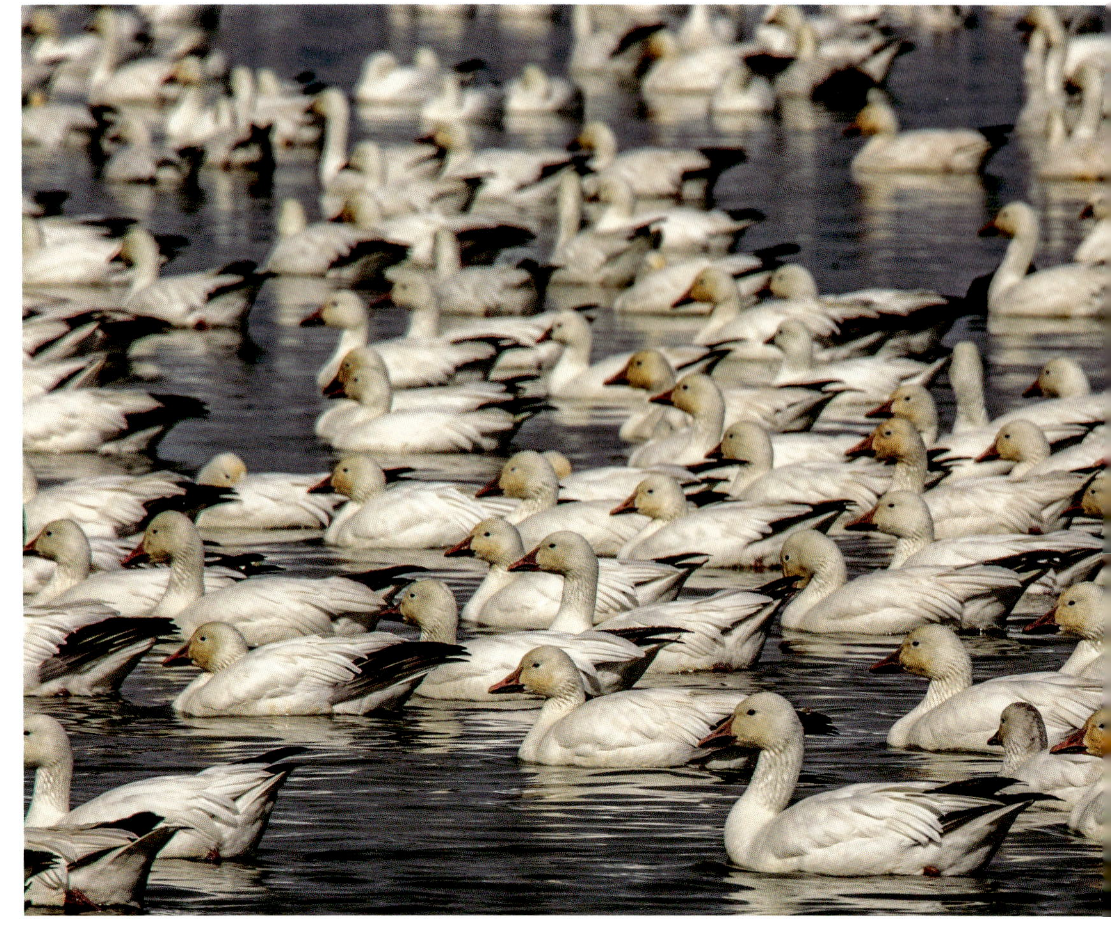

 Snow geese at Klamath National Wildlife Refuge. *Photo by Nick Viani.*

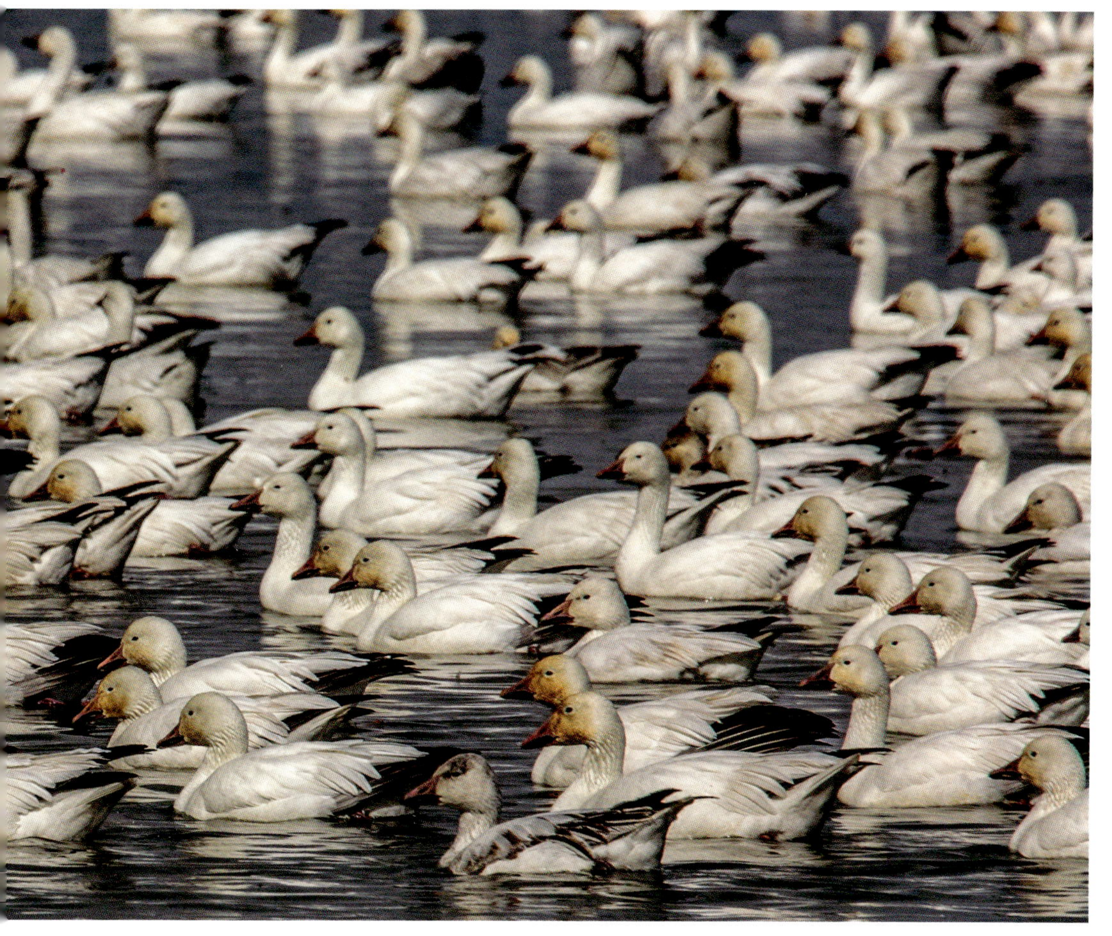

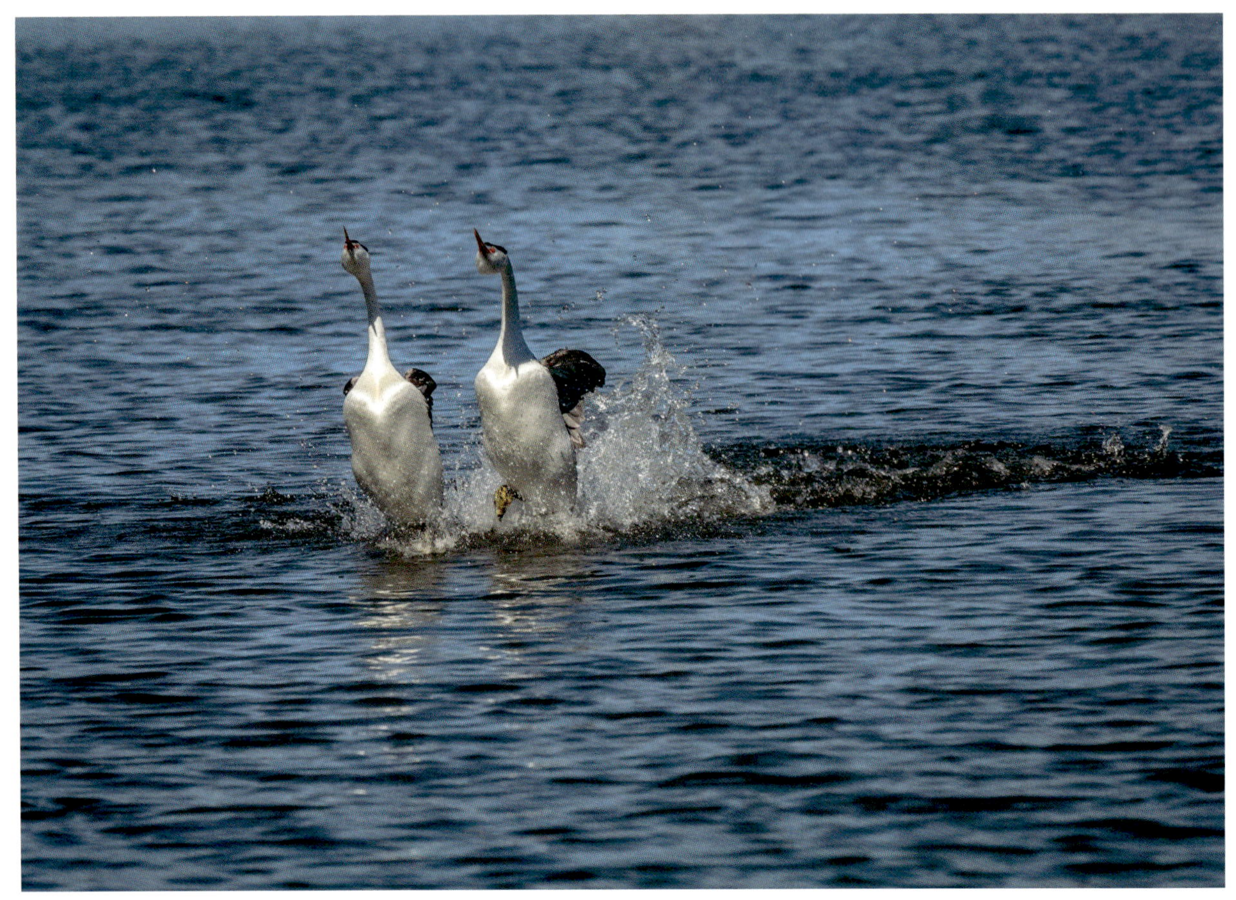

 Clark's grebe courtship dance at Klamath National Wildlife Refuge. *Photo by Nick Viani.*

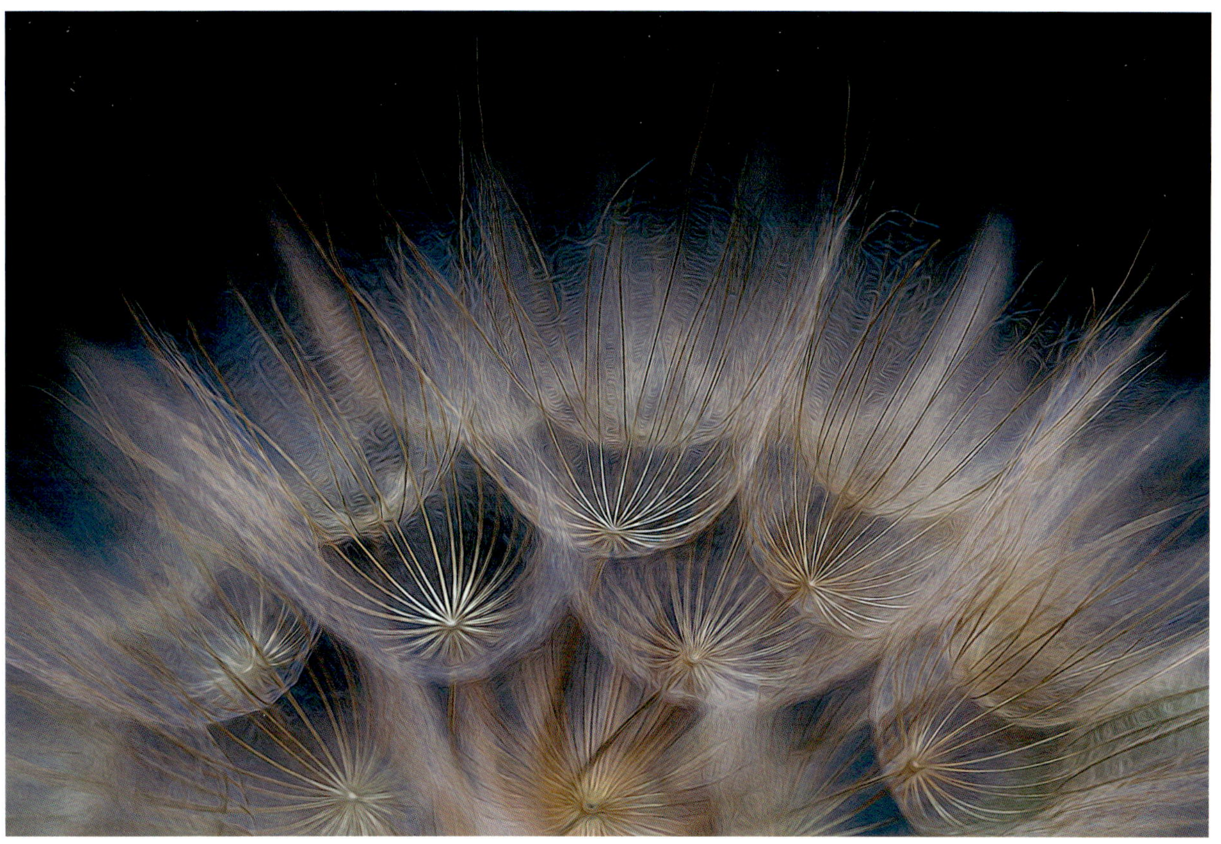

Dandelion whirls. *Photo by Alana Lynn Starkweather.*

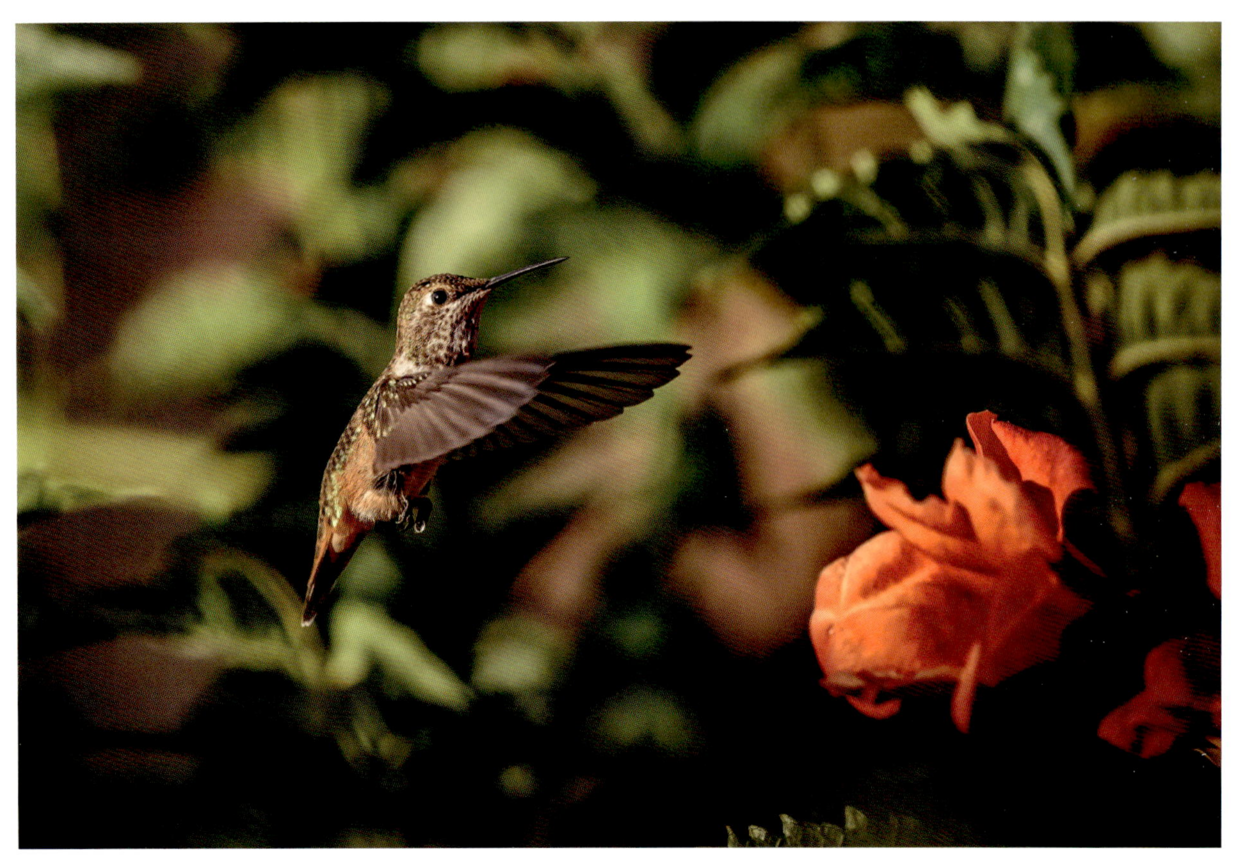

 Rufous hummingbird. *Photo by Nick Viani.*

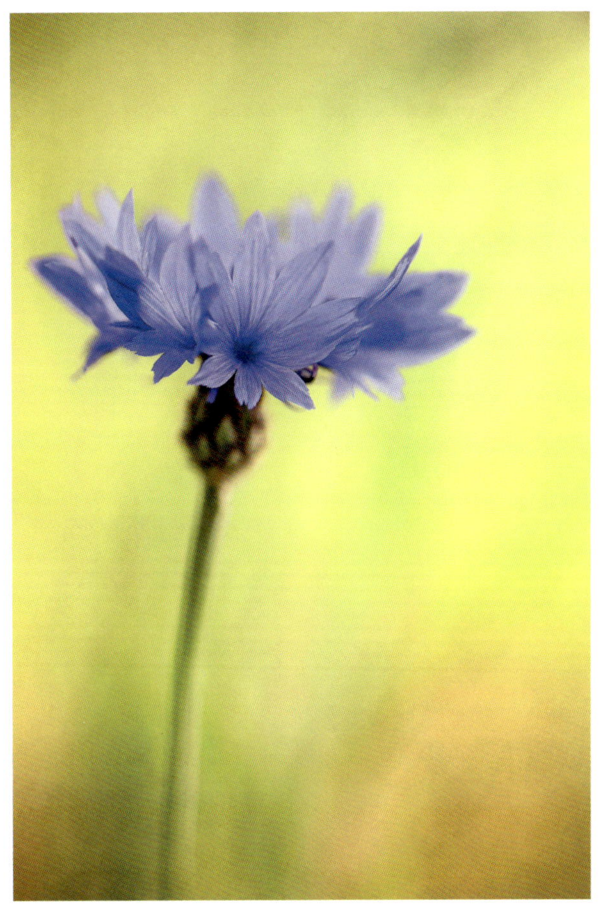

Bachelor button. *Photo by Julie Bonney.*

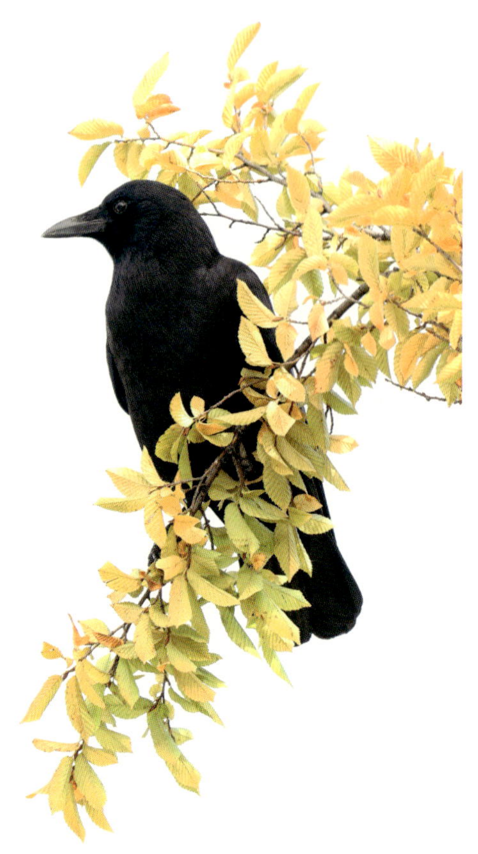

 Crow. *Photo by Dan Elster.*

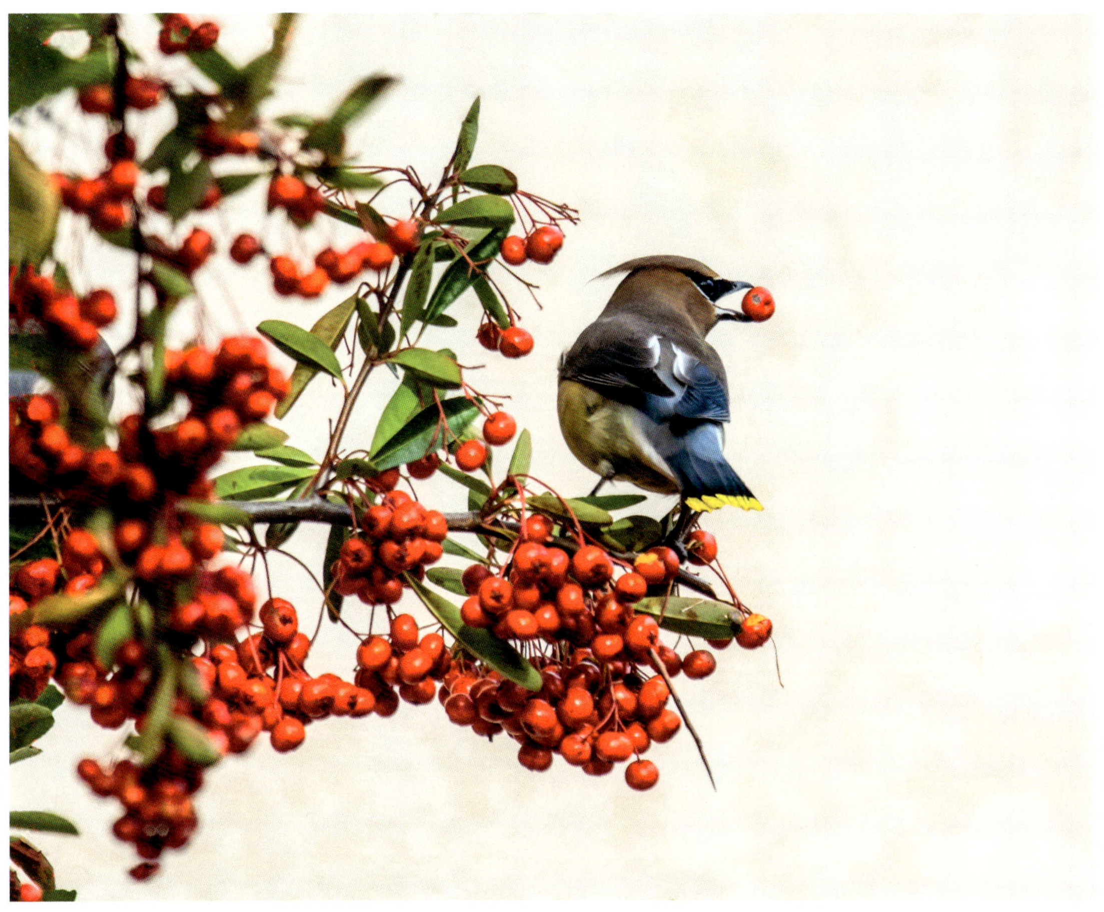

Cedar waxwing at Emigrant Lake. *Photo by George F. Peterson.*

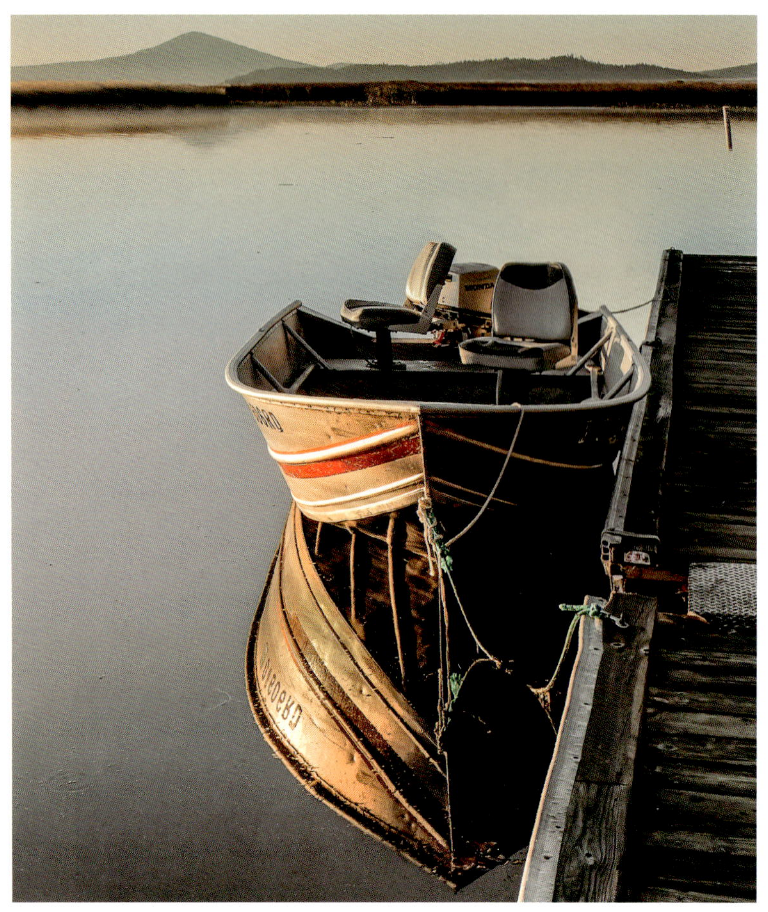

 Boat reflection at Klamath Lake. *Photo by Kate Geary.*

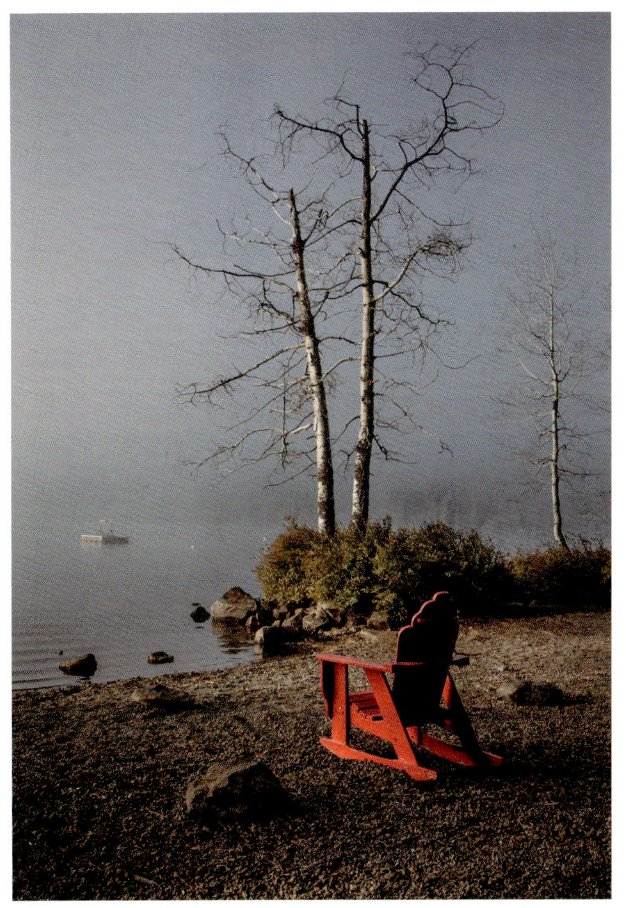

Lake of the Woods. *Photo by Kate Geary.*

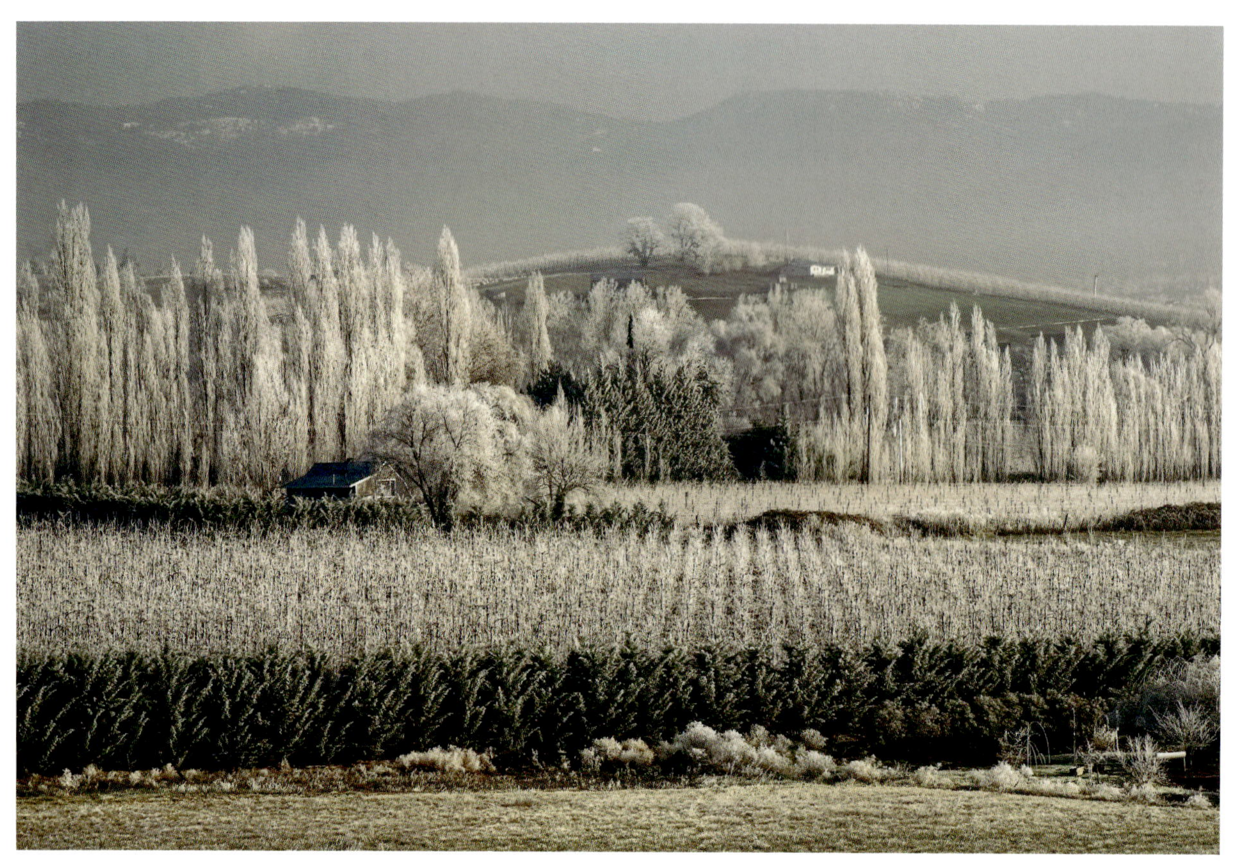

 Phoenix orchards. *Photo by Jay Newman.*

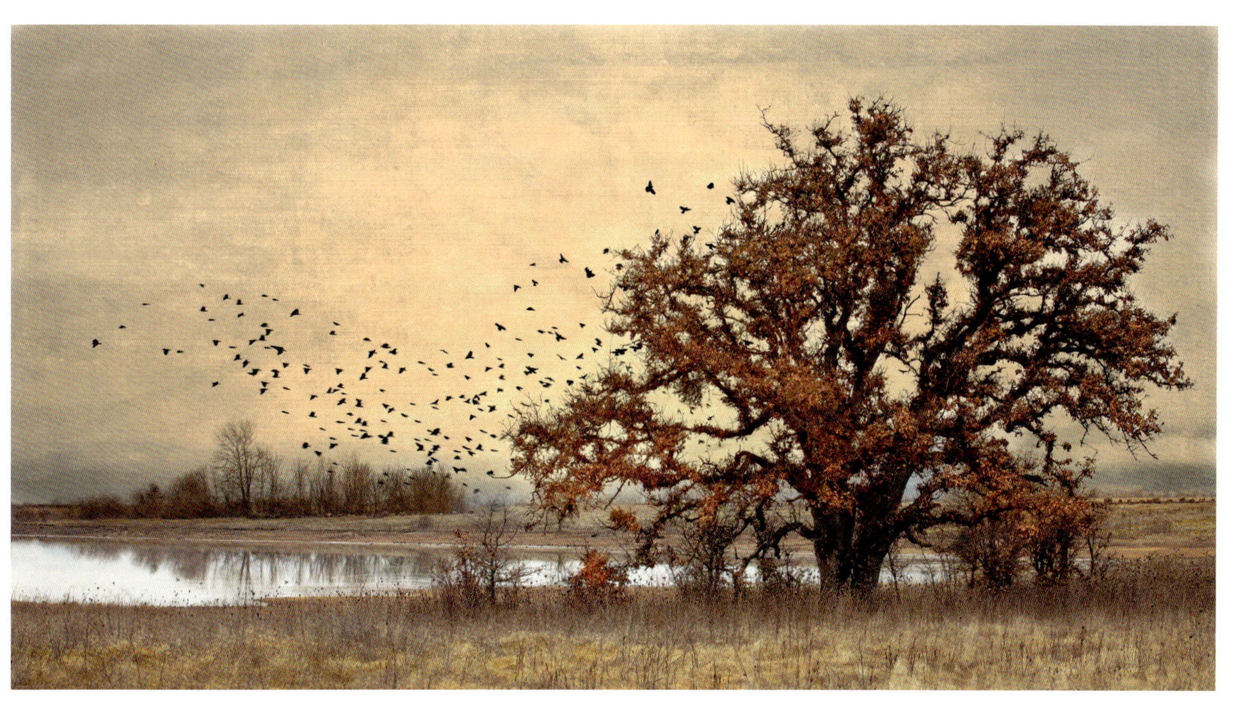

Agate Lake near Medford. *Photo by Julie Bonney.*

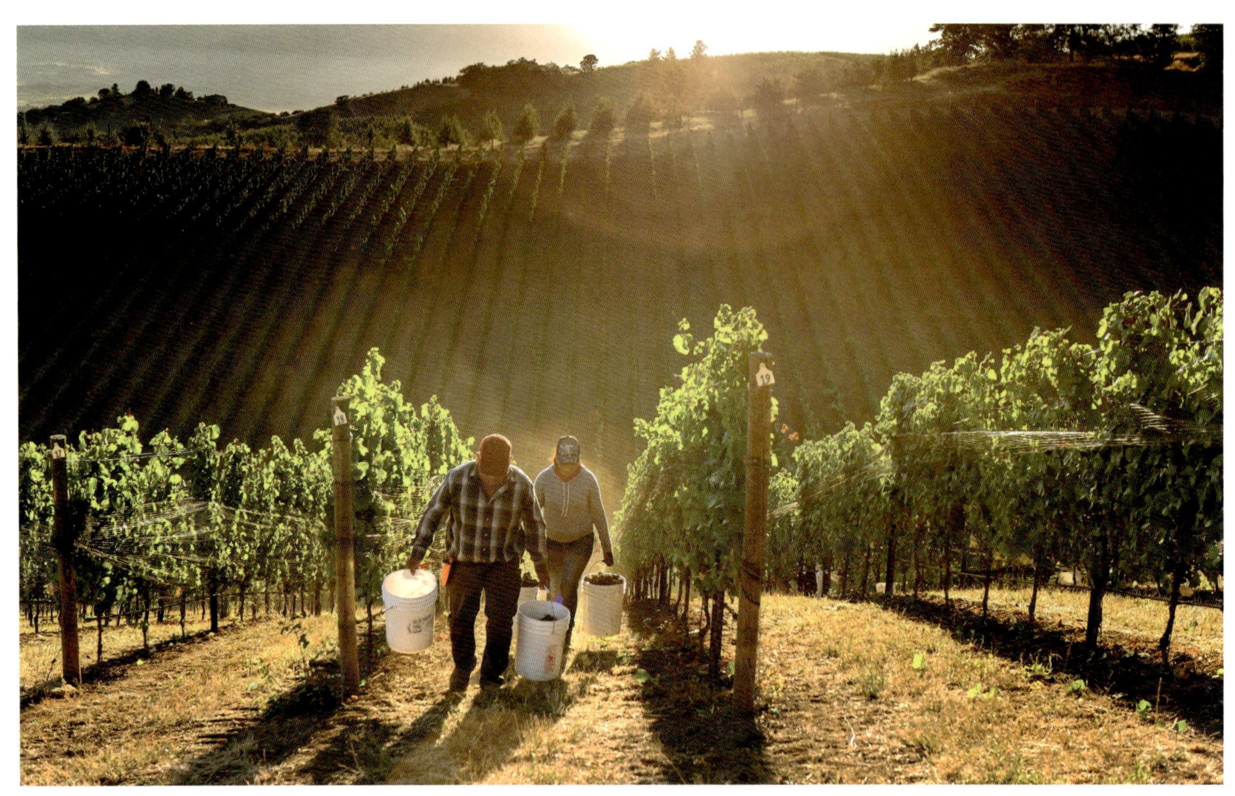

 Pinot noir harvest, Jacksonville. *Photo by Jim Craven.*

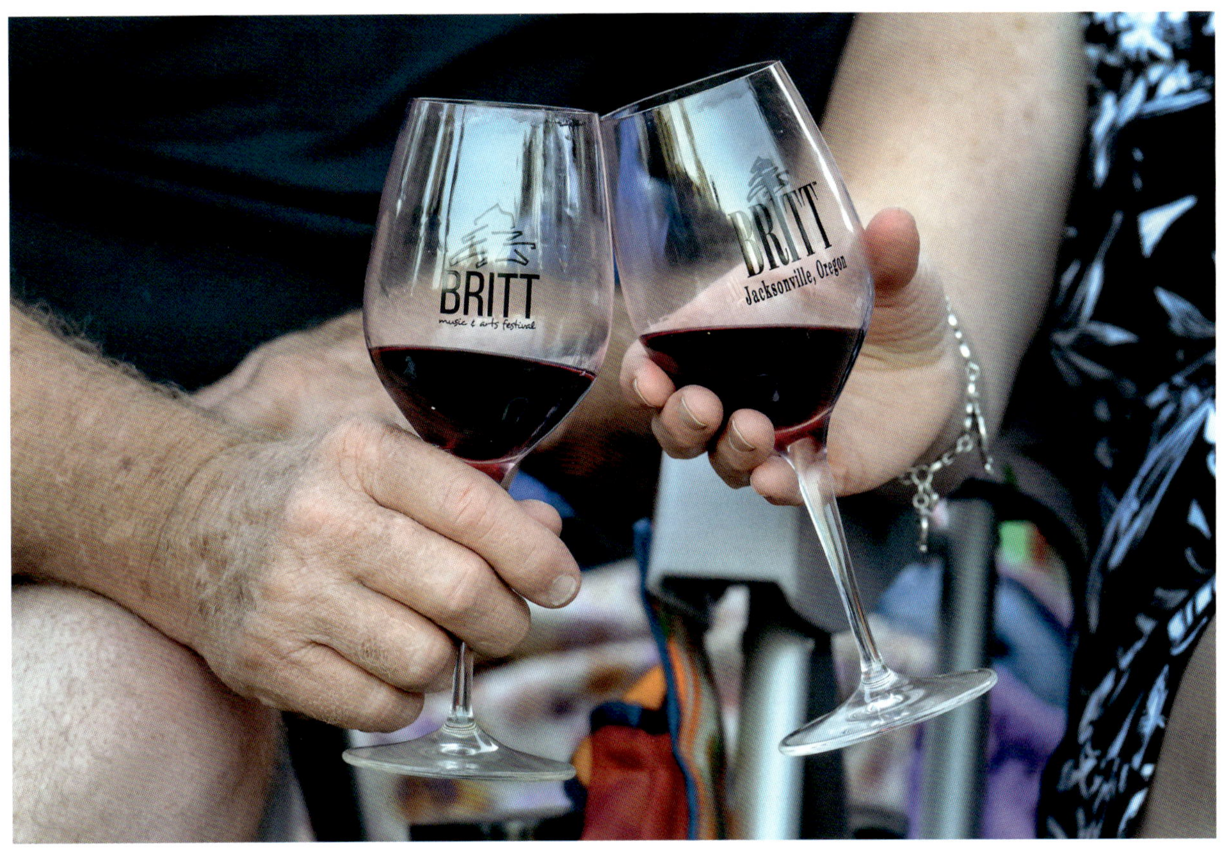

The Britt Festival in Jacksonville has been a performing-arts festival since 1963. *Photo by Jim Craven.*

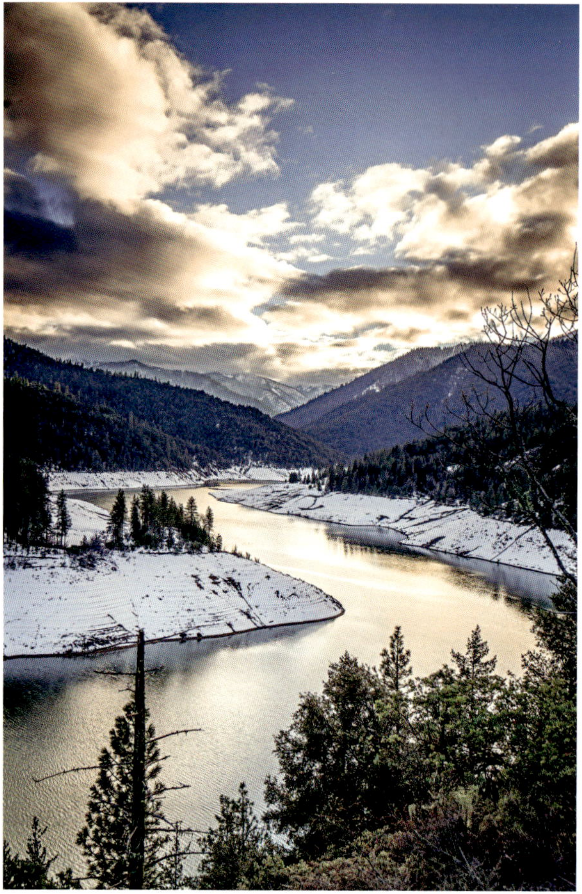

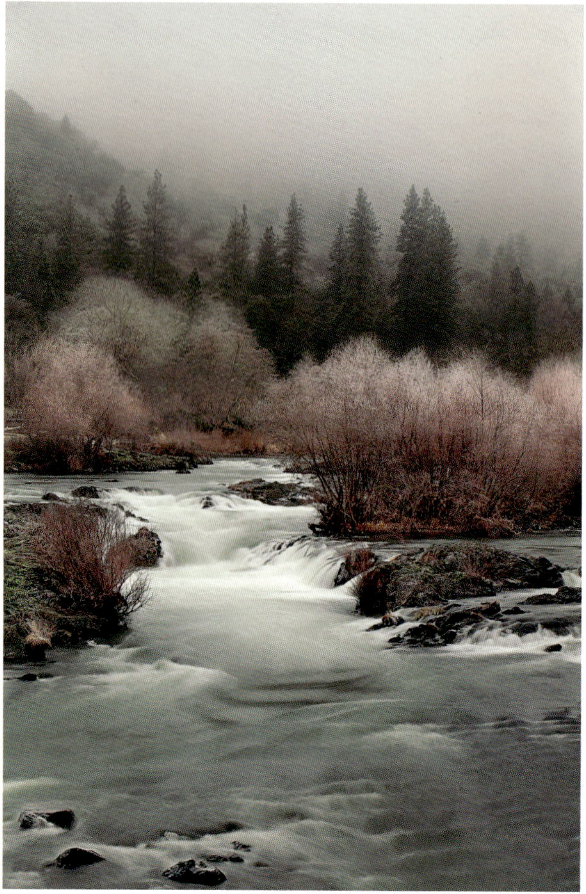

Applegate Lake. *Photo by Alana Lynn Starkweather.* • Rogue River. *Photo by Julie Bonney.*

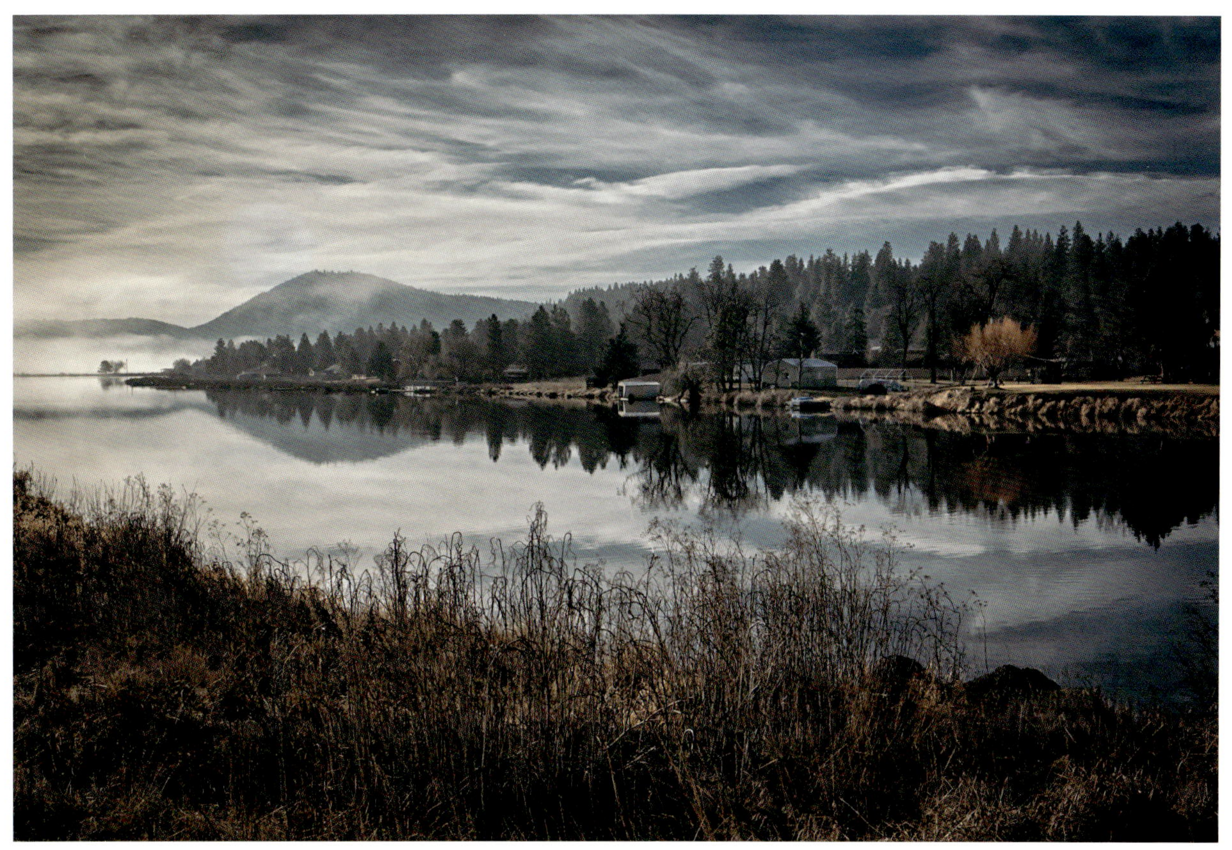

Klamath Lake. *Photo by Barbara Tricarico.*

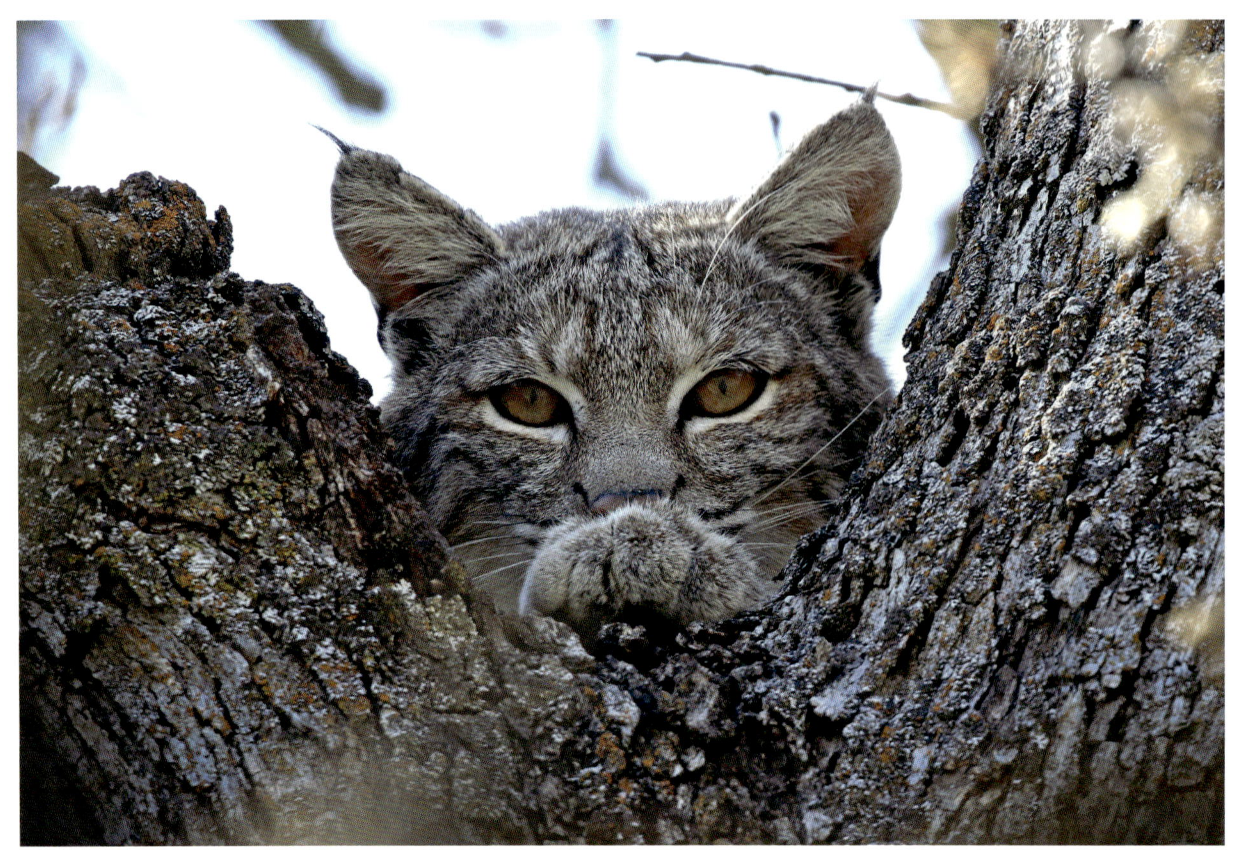

 Bobcat. *Photo by Dan Elster.*

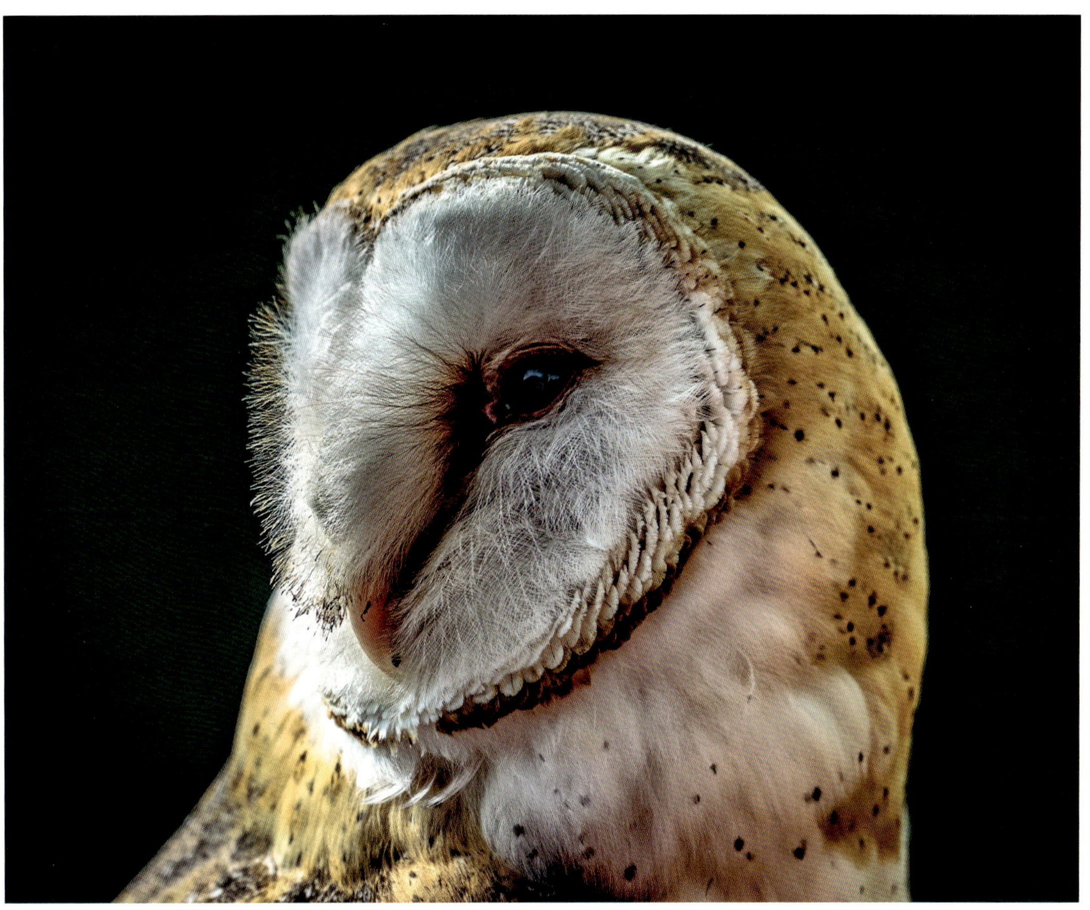

Barn owl at North Mountain Park, Ashland. *Photo by Nick Viani.*

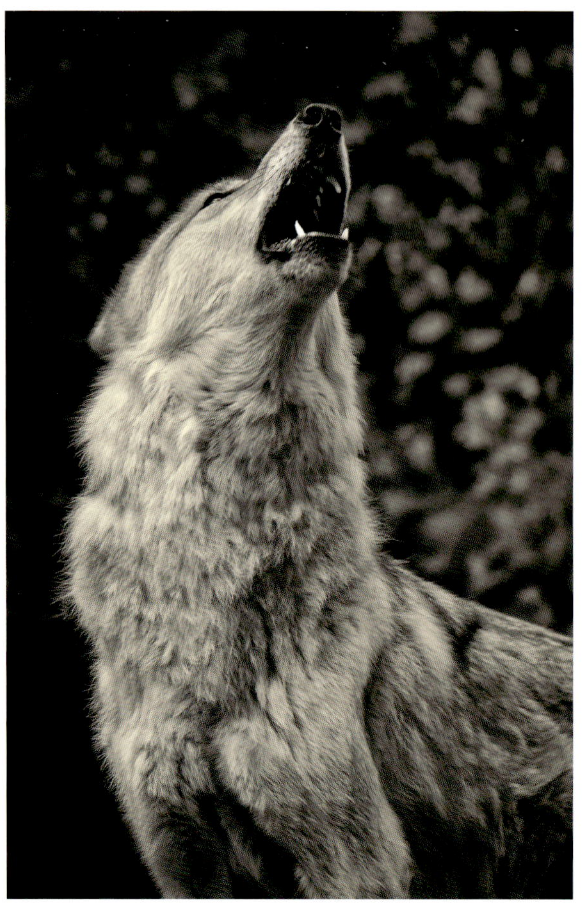

 Howling wolf at Wildlife Images Rehabilitation and Education Center. *Photo by Judy Benson LaNier.*

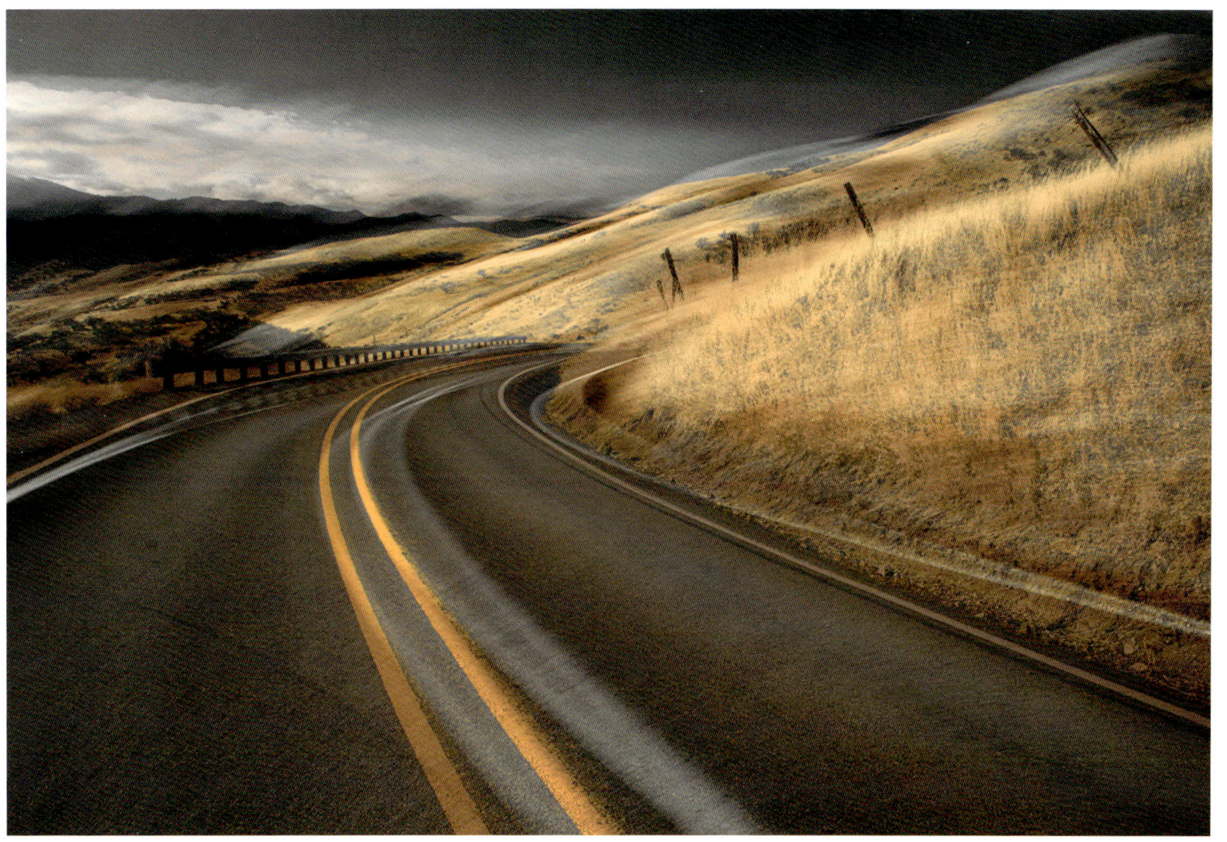

Indian Memorial Road, Ashland. *Photo by David Lorenz Winston.*

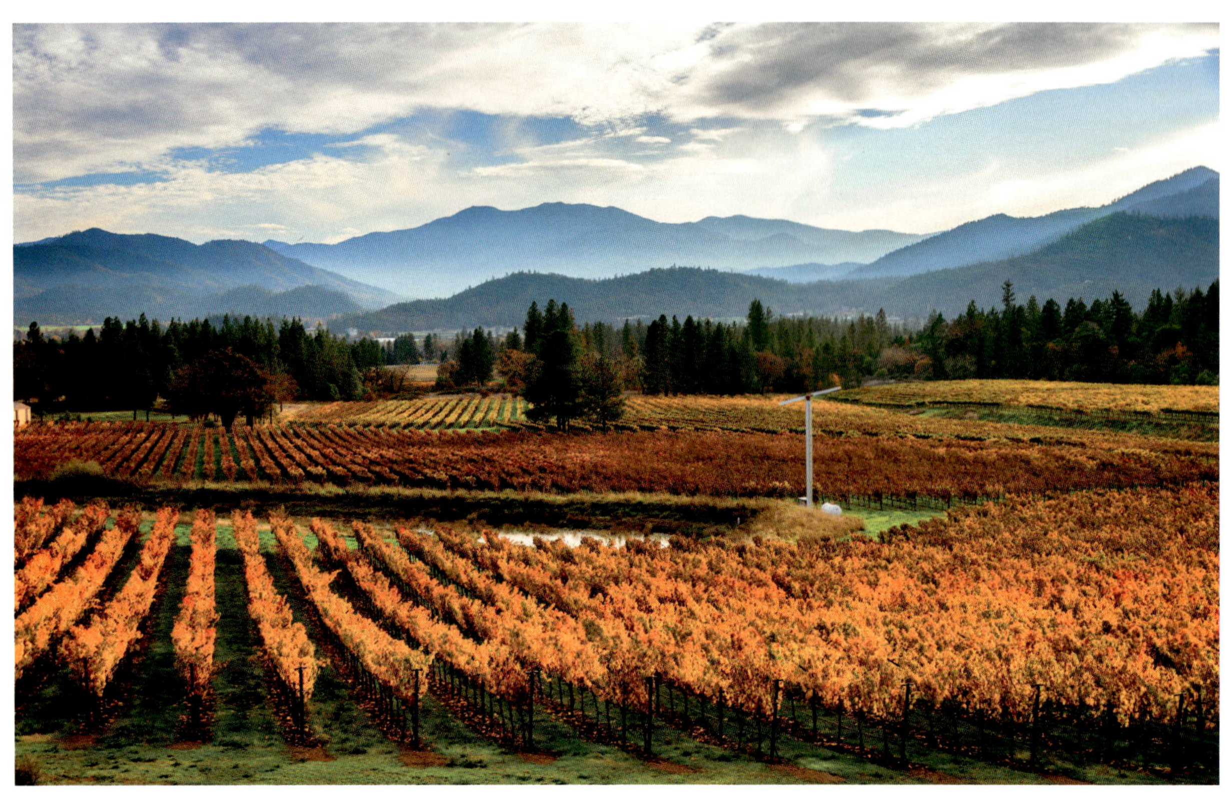

 Rogue Valley vineyards. *Photo by Nomeca Hartwell.*

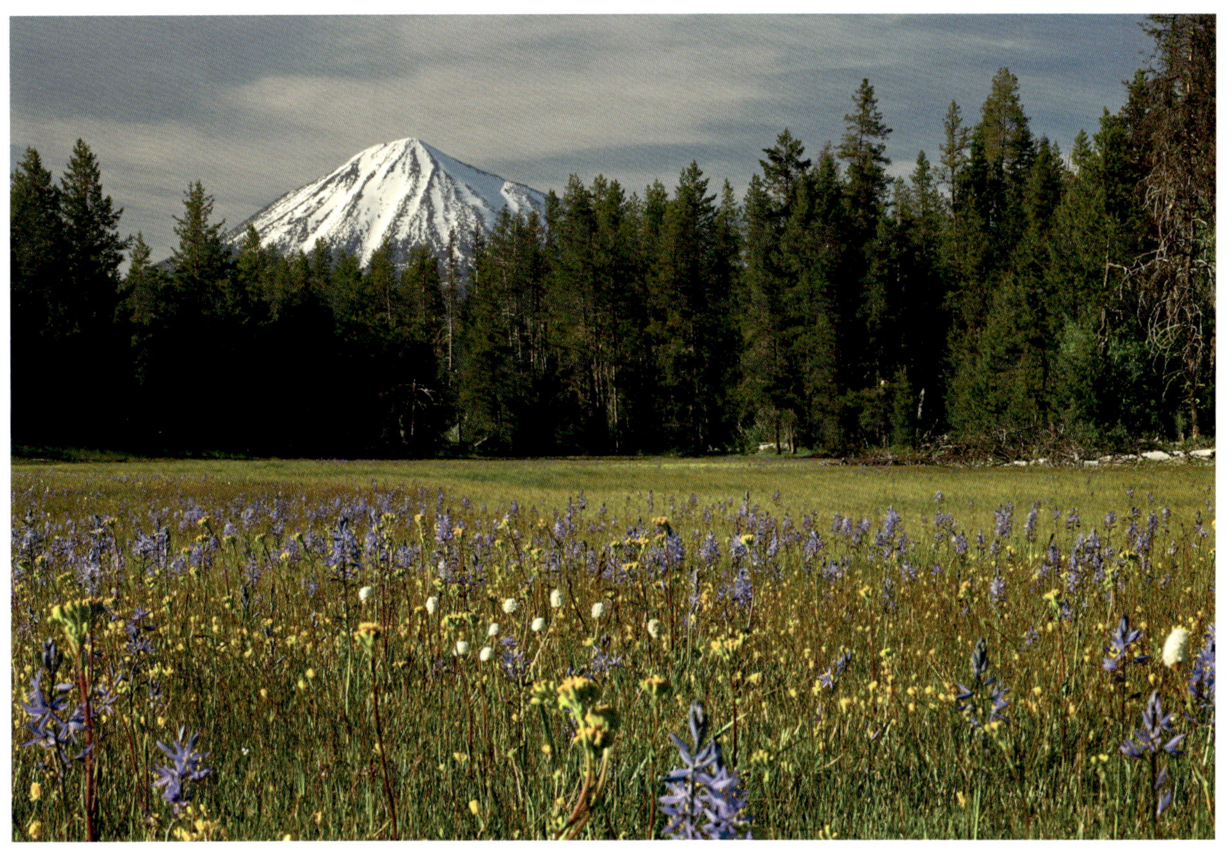

Mount McLaughlin and wildflowers. *Photo by Jay Newman.*

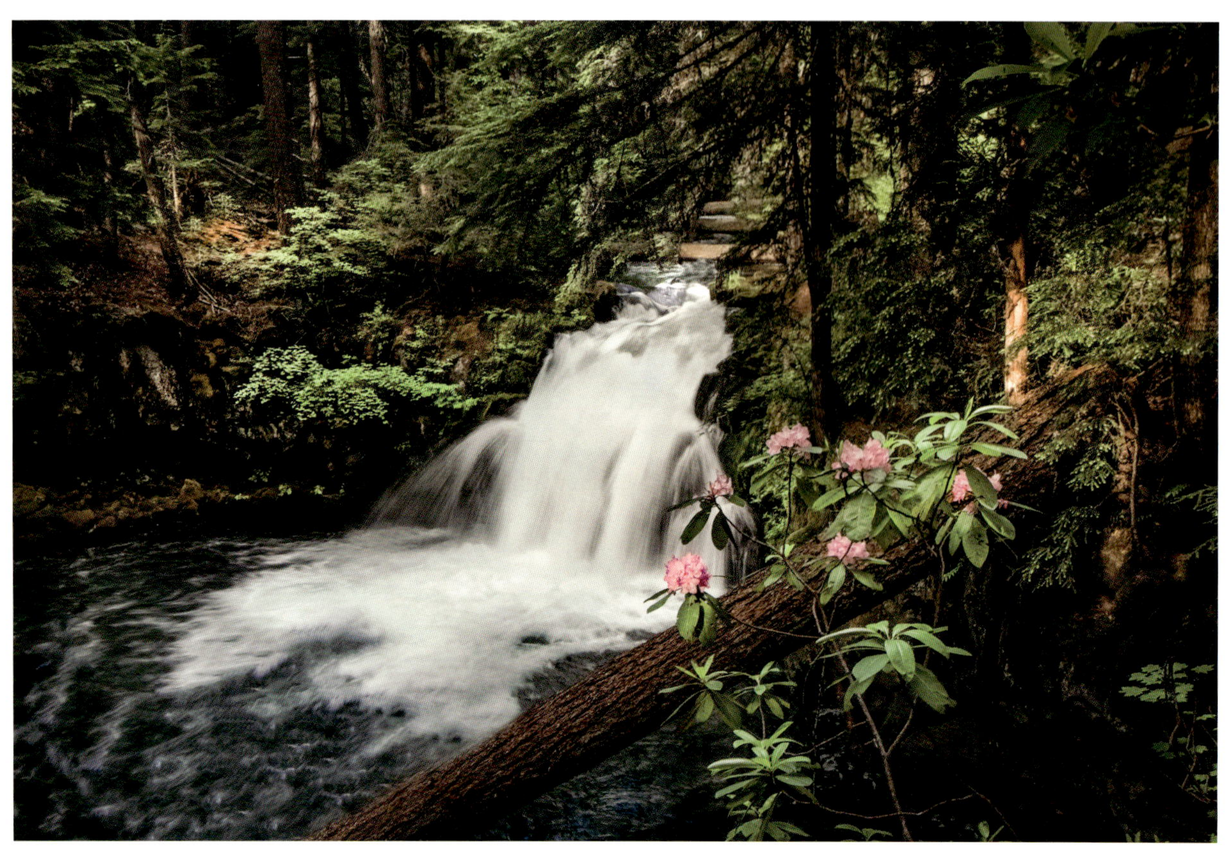

 Whitehorse Falls, Umpqua National Forest. *Photo by Sue Stendebach.*

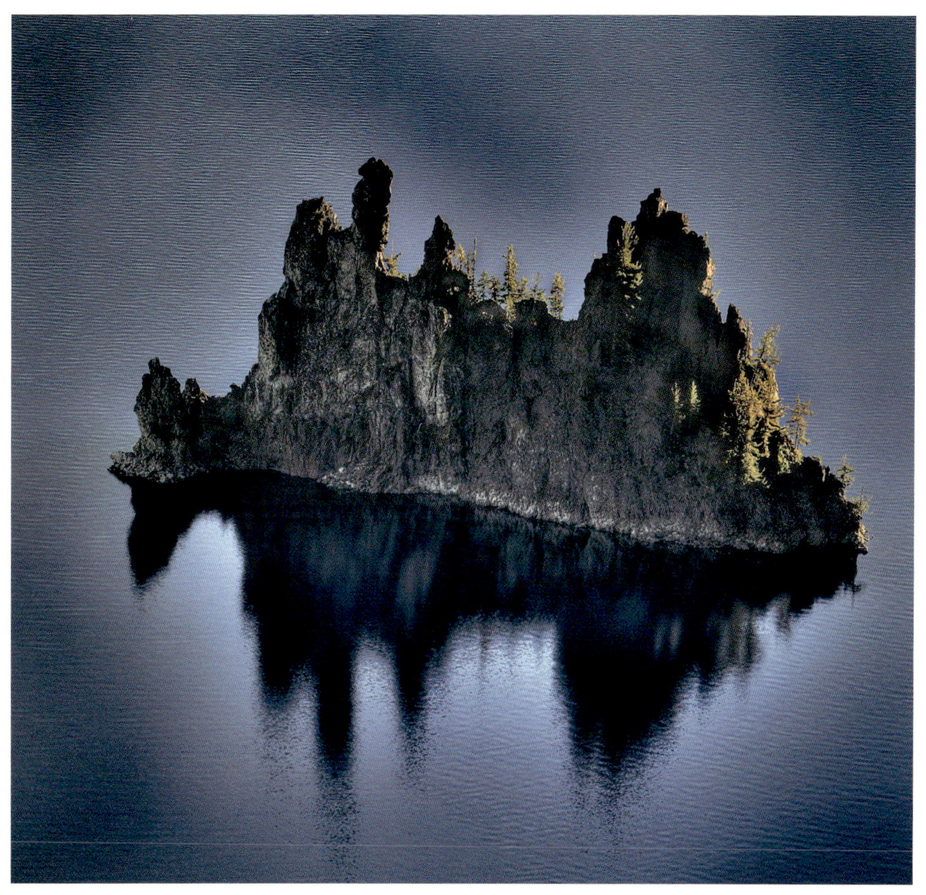

Phantom ship at Crater Lake. *Photo by Neal R. Thompson.*

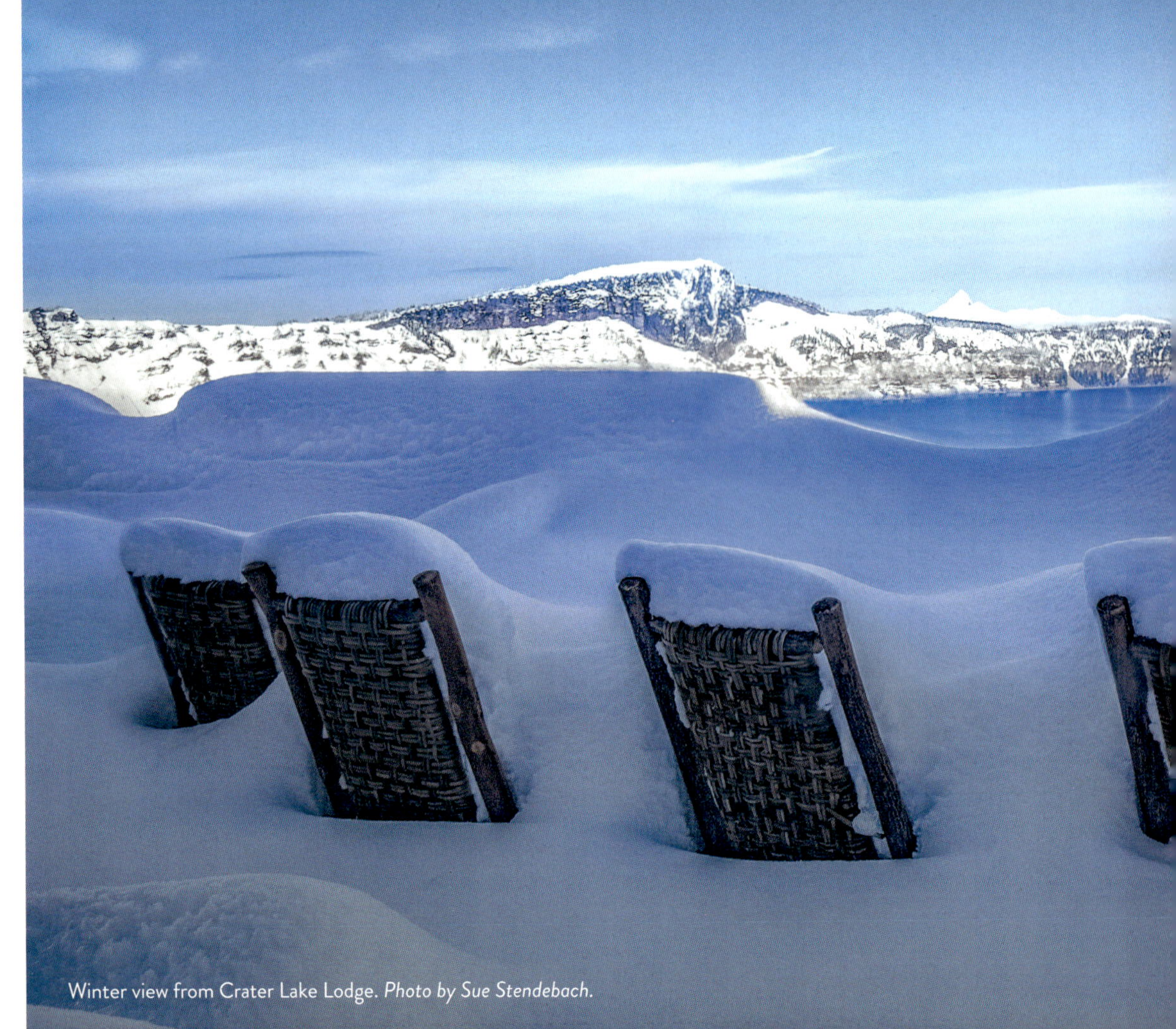

Winter view from Crater Lake Lodge. *Photo by Sue Stendebach.*

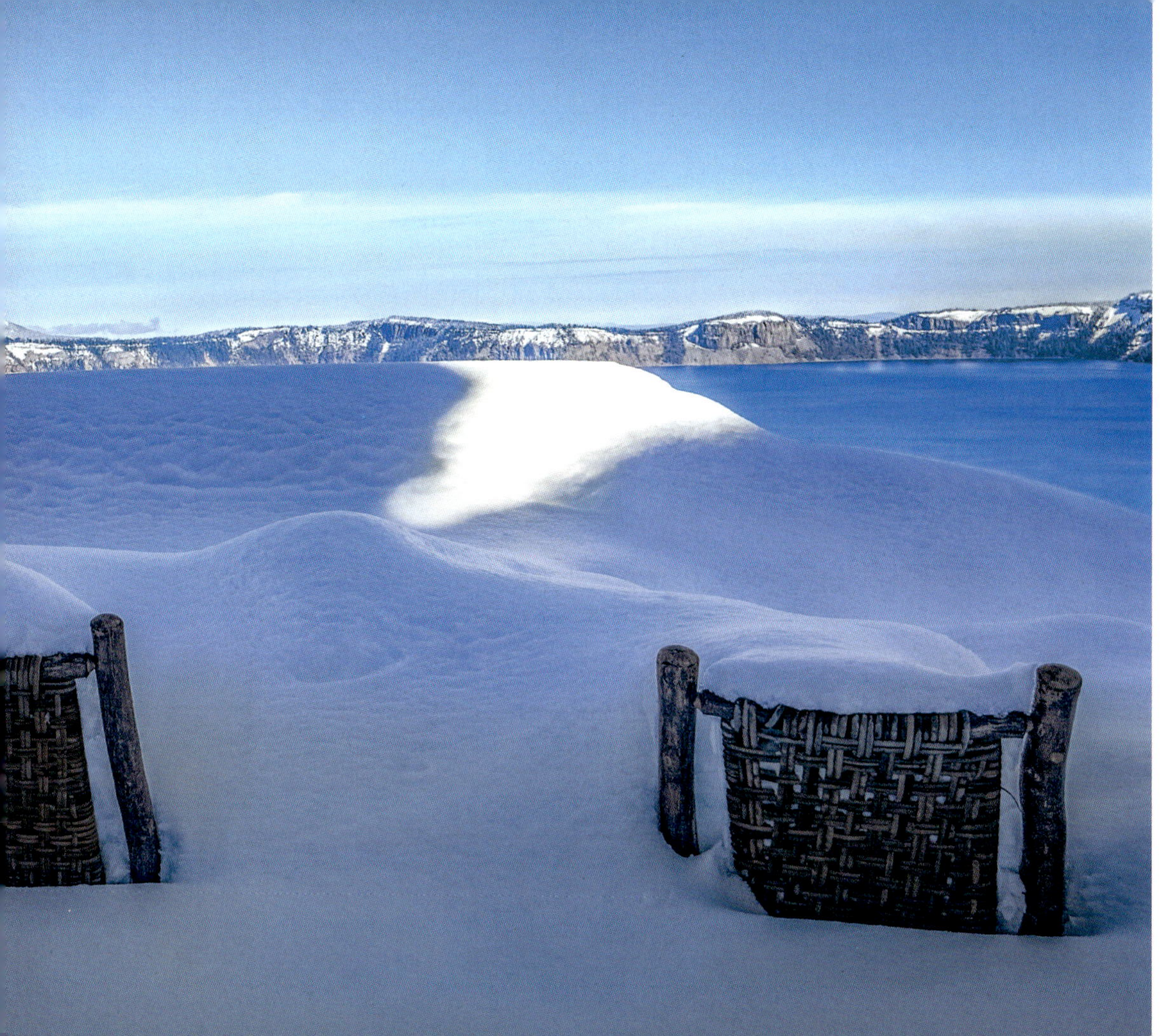

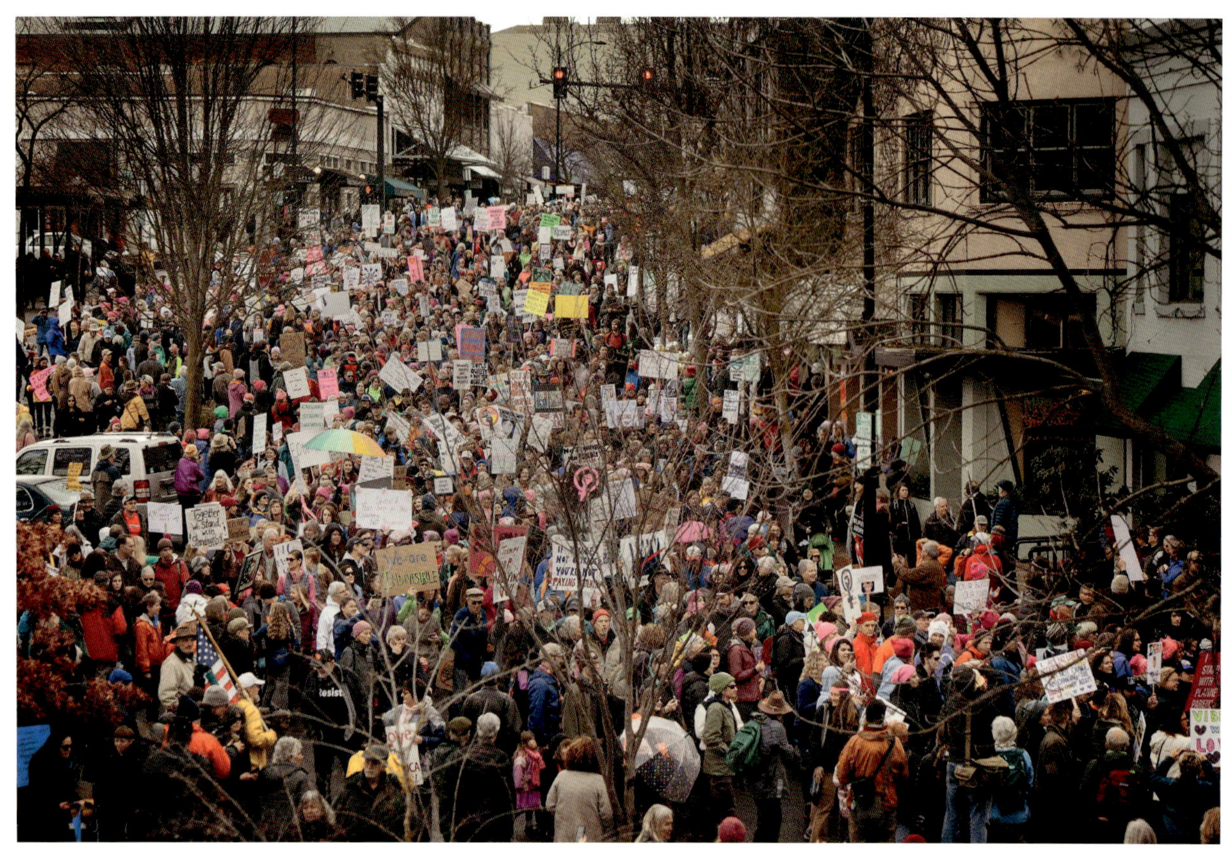

 Downtown Ashland's community spirit and activism shows during several parades and rallies each year on Main Street. *Photo by John Kirk.*

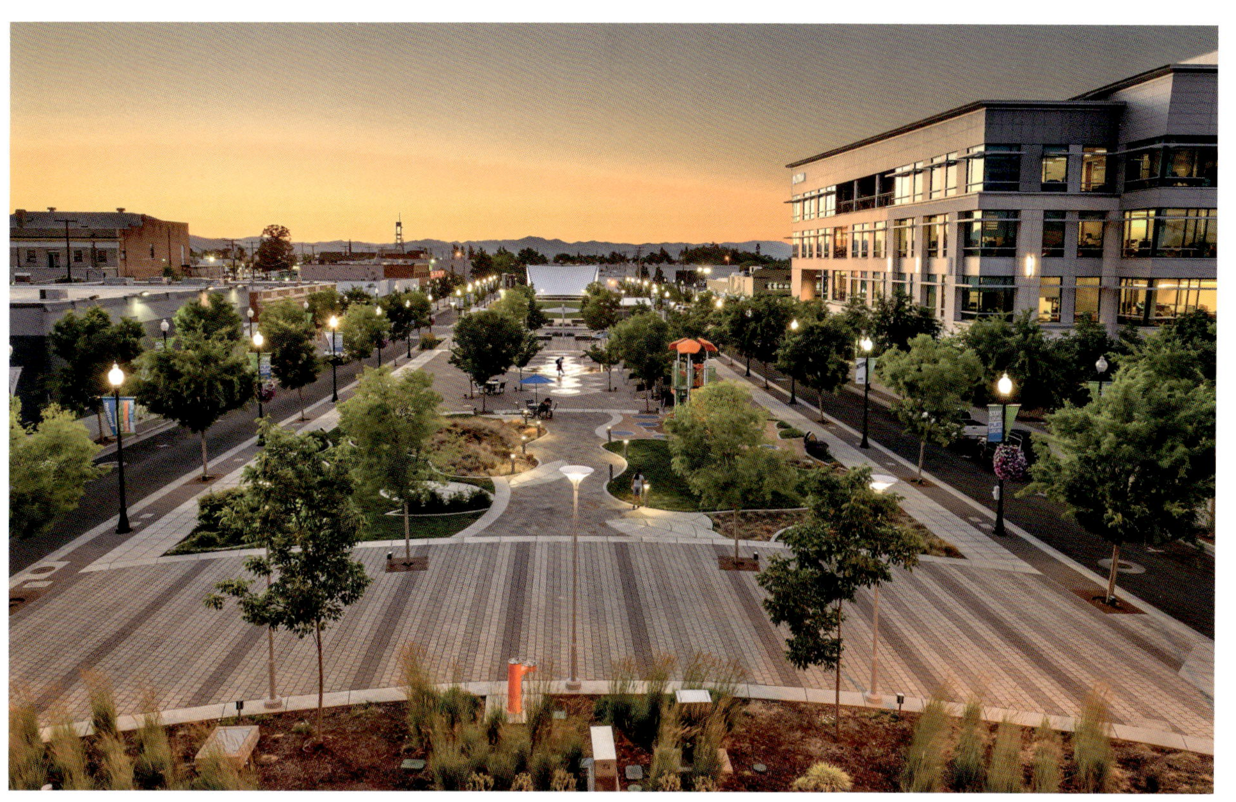

Pear Blossom Park is a vibrant gathering spot in Medford. It hosts music concerts, a Christmas tree lighting, rallies, and community events. *Photo by Jim Craven.*

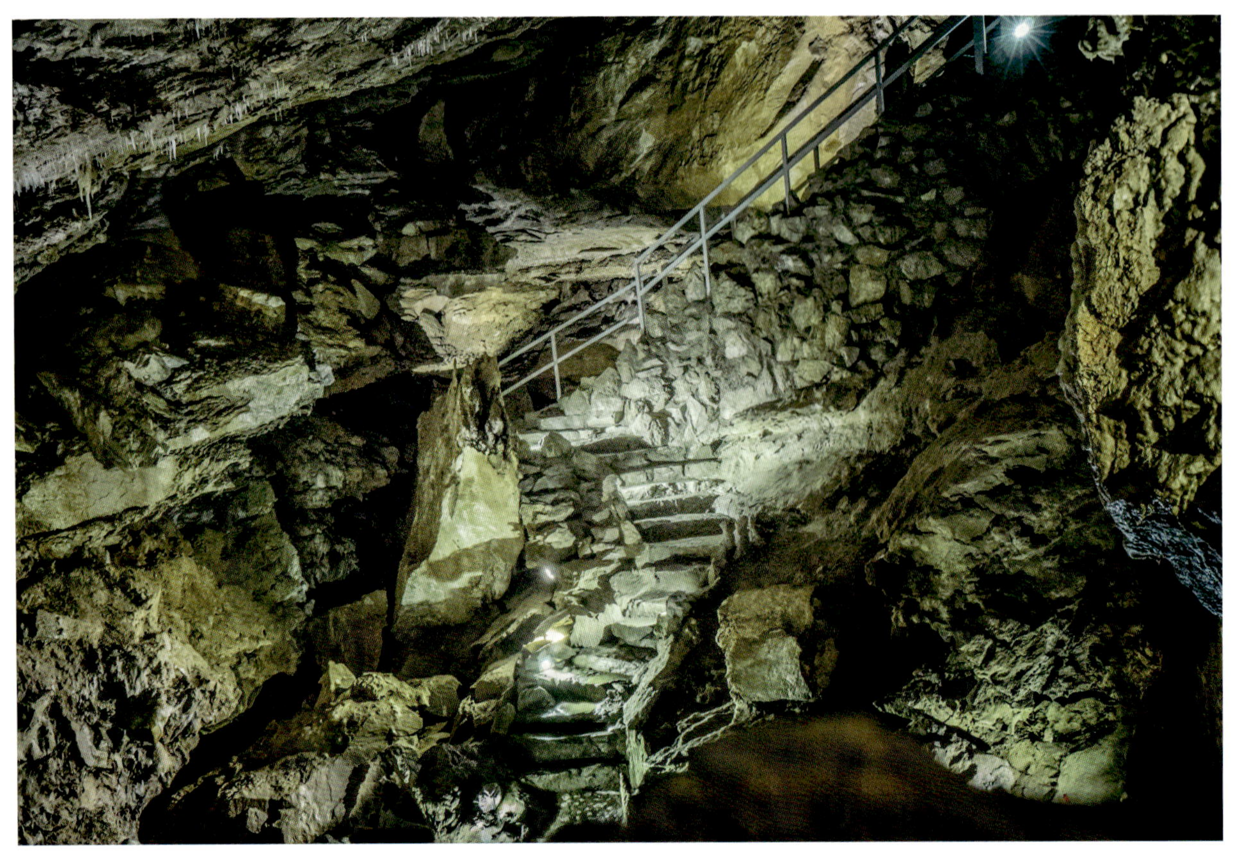

 Oregon Caves, Cave Junction. *Photo by Randy Bryan.*

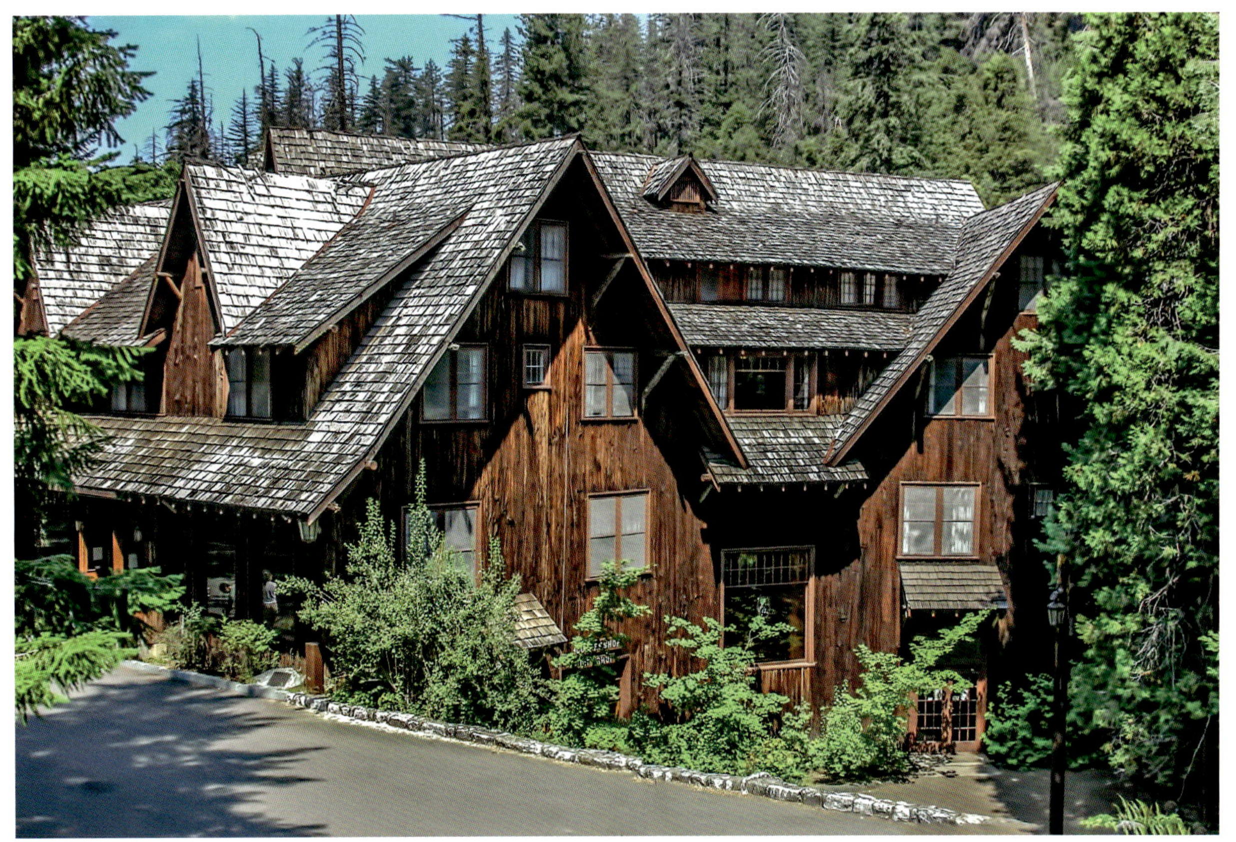

Oregon Caves Chateau, Cave Junction, built in 1934. *Photo by George F. Peterson.*

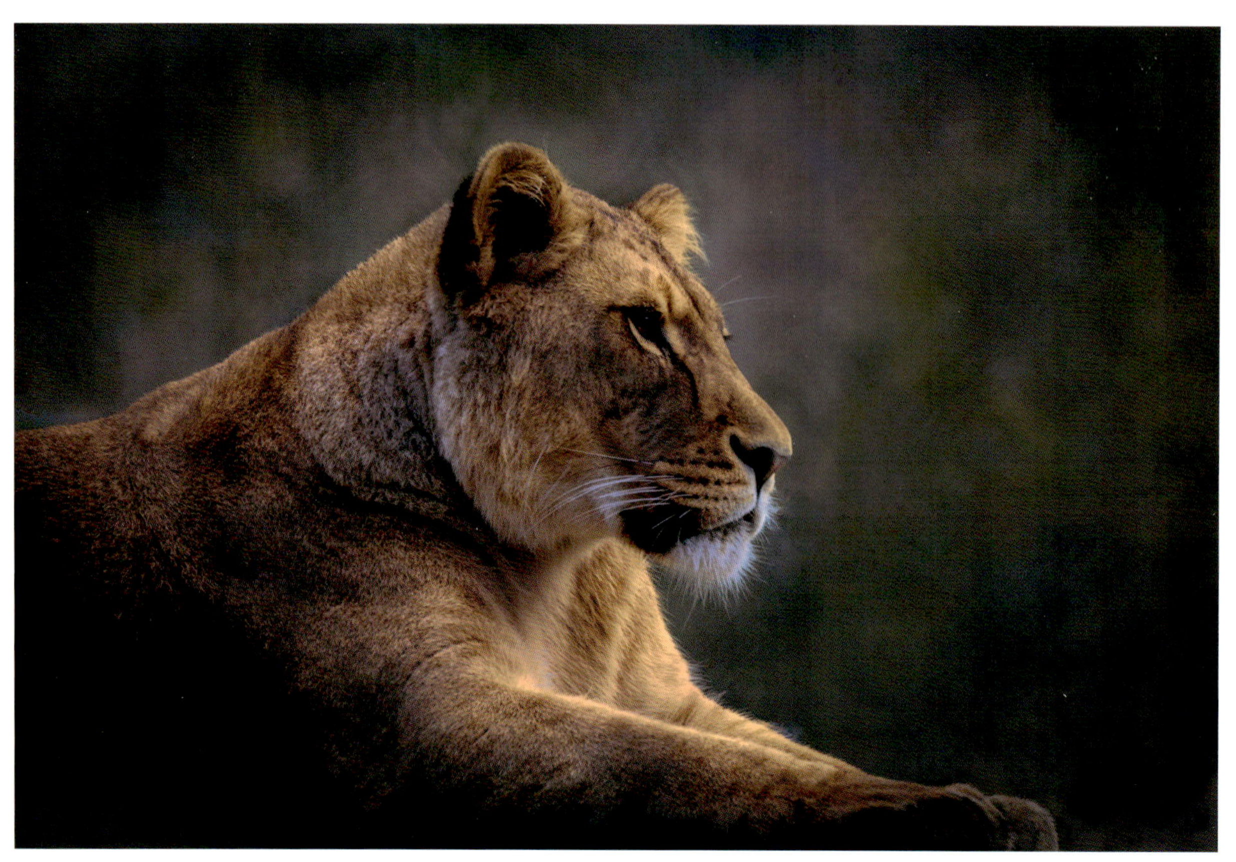

 Lion at Wildlife Safari, Winston. *Photo by Alana Lynn Starkweather.*

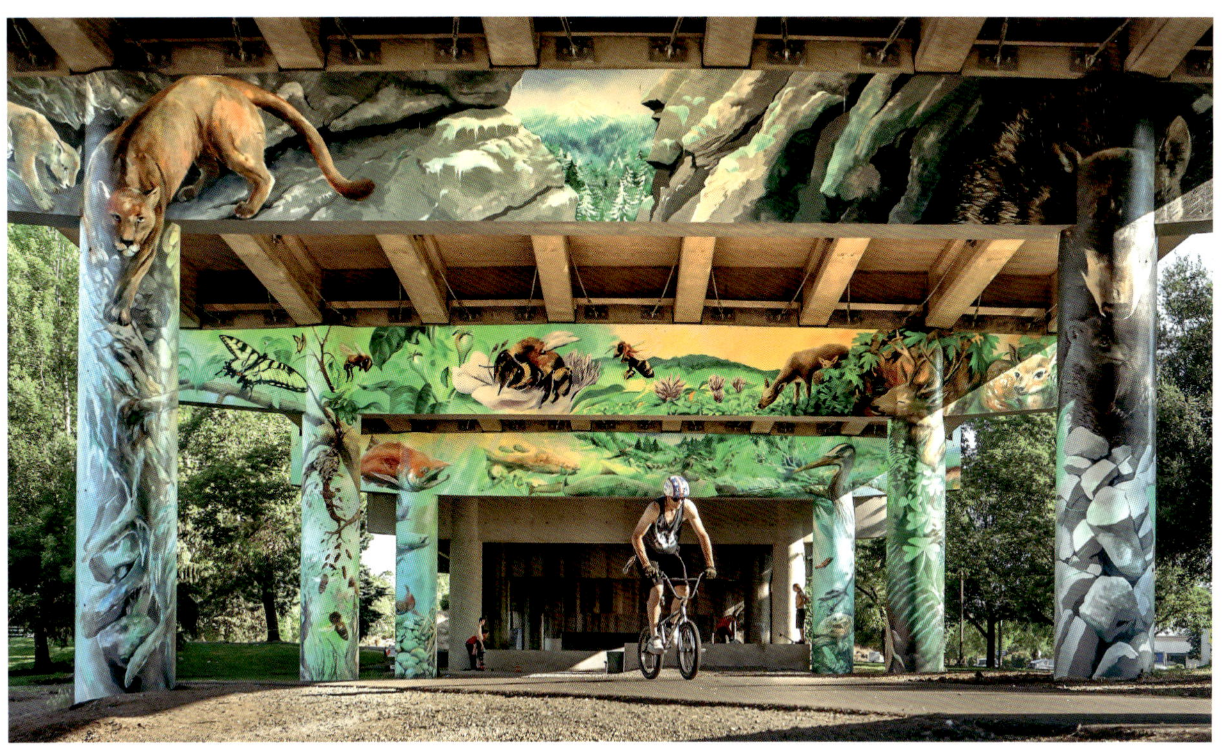

Hawthorne Park, Medford. *Photo by Jim Craven.*

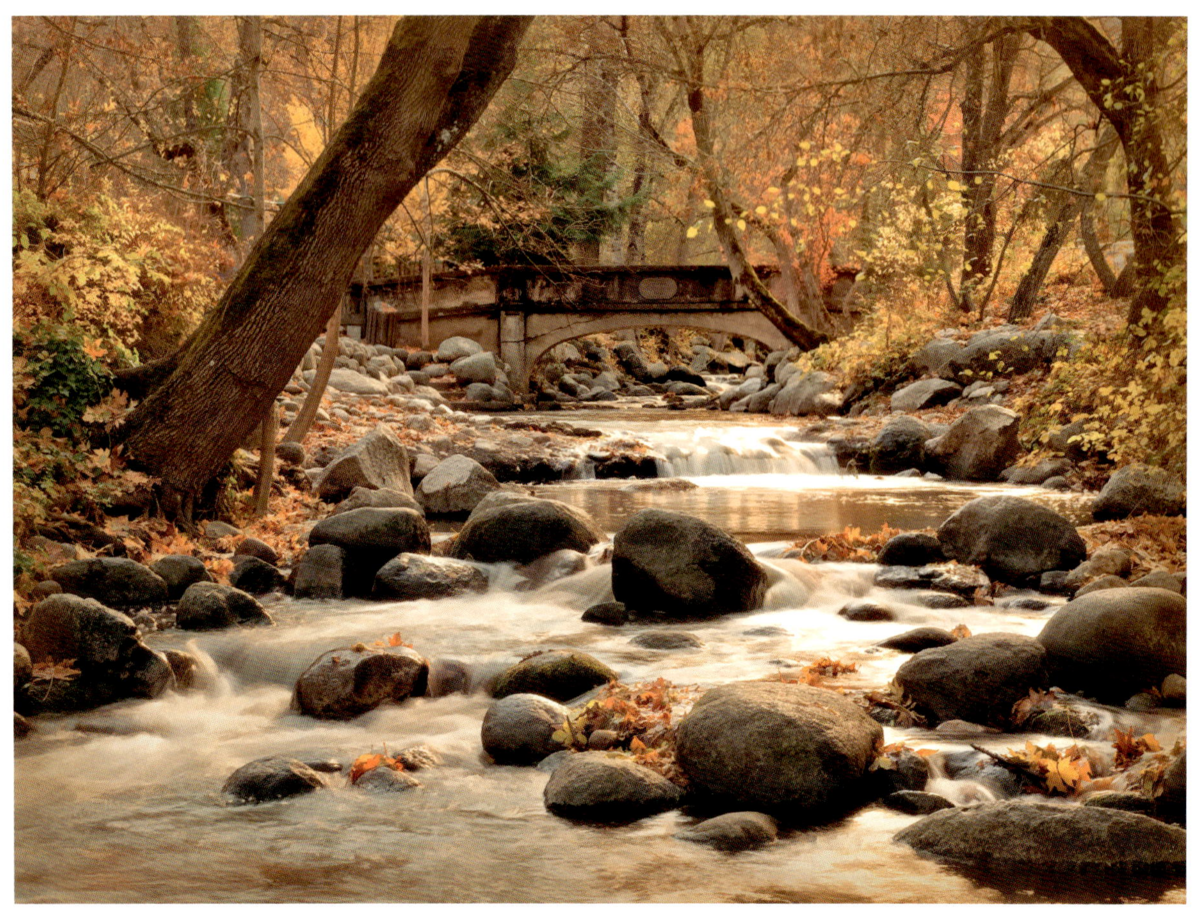

 Ashland Creek in Lithia Park, Ashland. *Photo by Vivian McAleavey.*

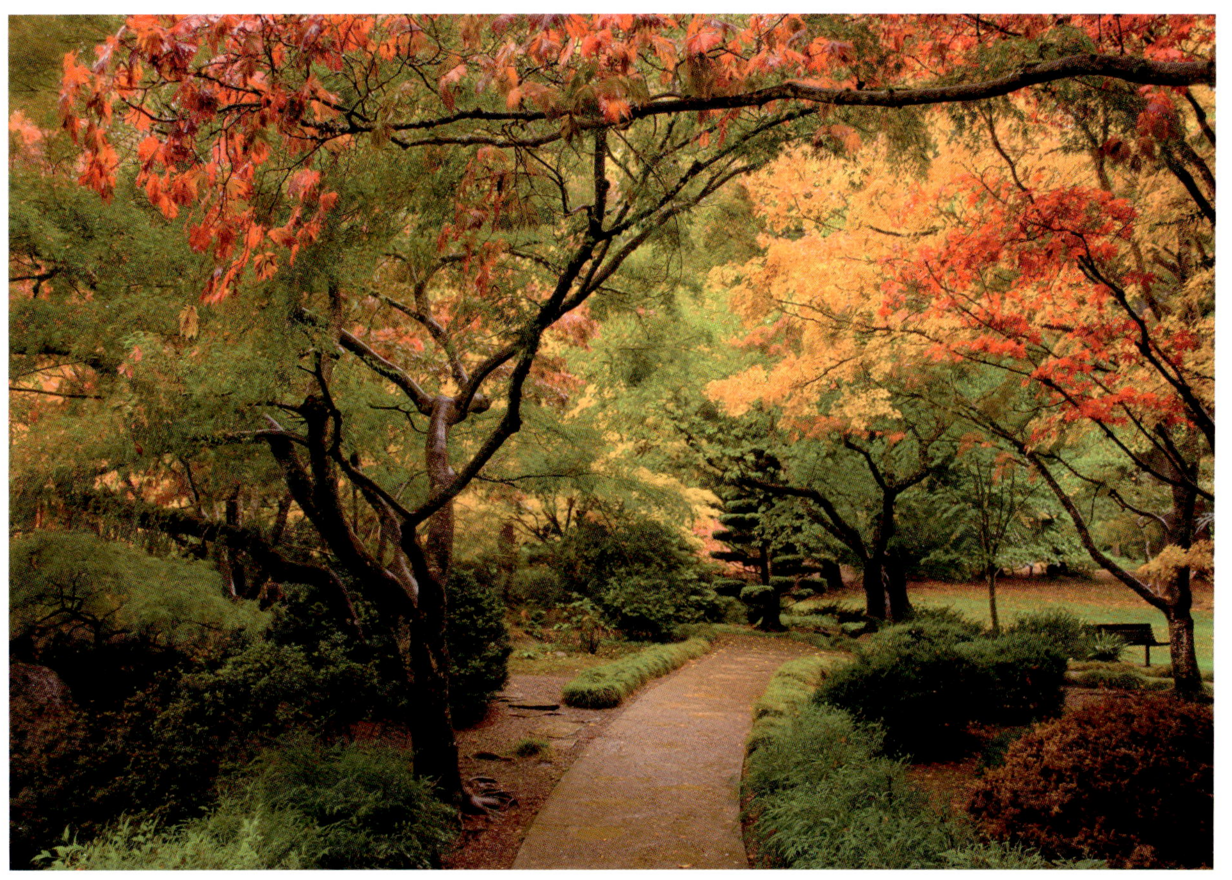

Lithia Park's Japanese Garden, Ashland. *Photo by Clem Paslack.*

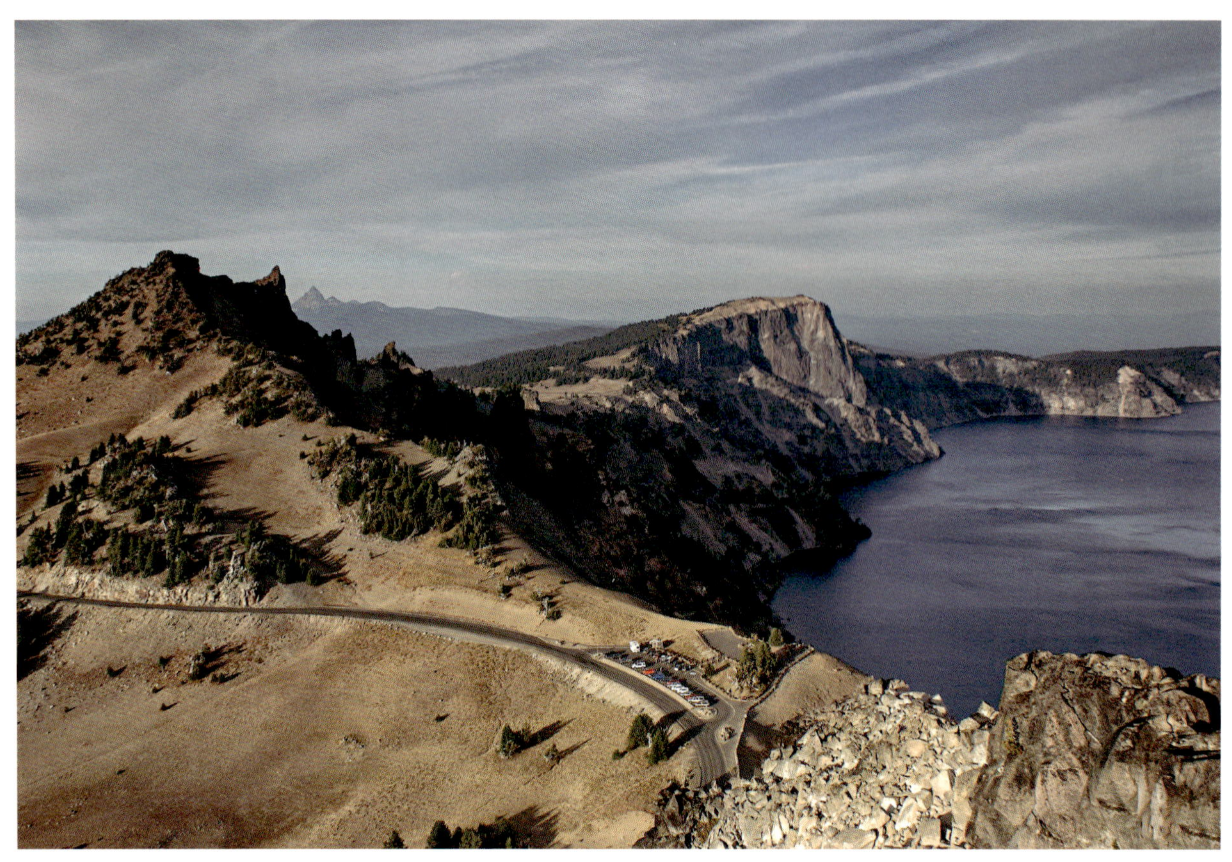

 Crater Lake from Watchman Peak Trail. *Photo by Ken Deveney.*

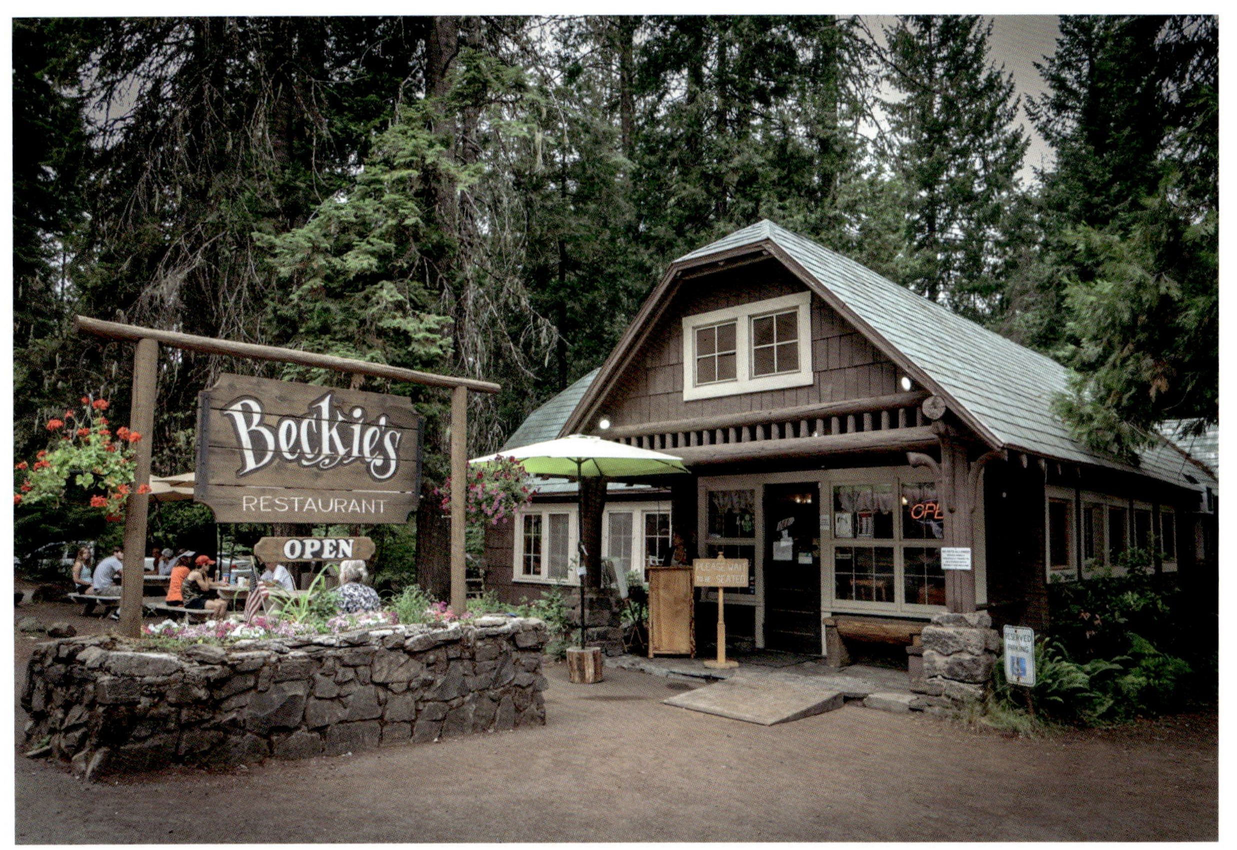

Beckie's Restaurant, built in 1926, Union Creek. *Photo by Barbara Tricarico.*

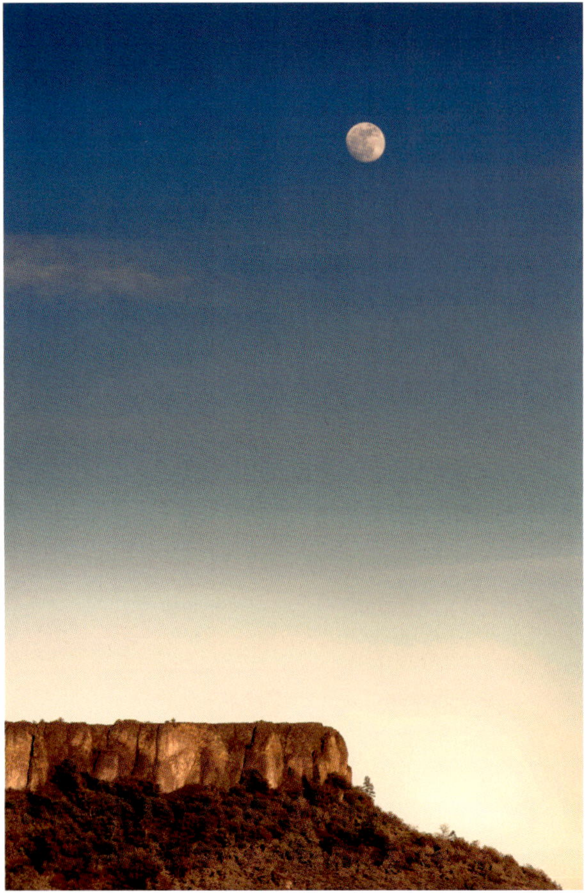

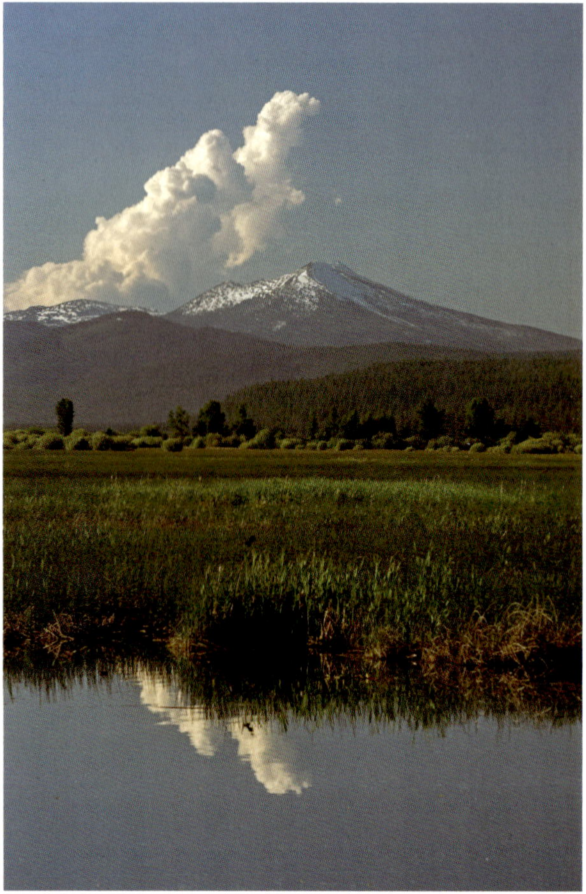

 Lower Table Rock near Central Point. *Photo by Jim Craven.* • Mount Scott, Crater Lake National Park's highest point. *Photo by Jay Newman.*

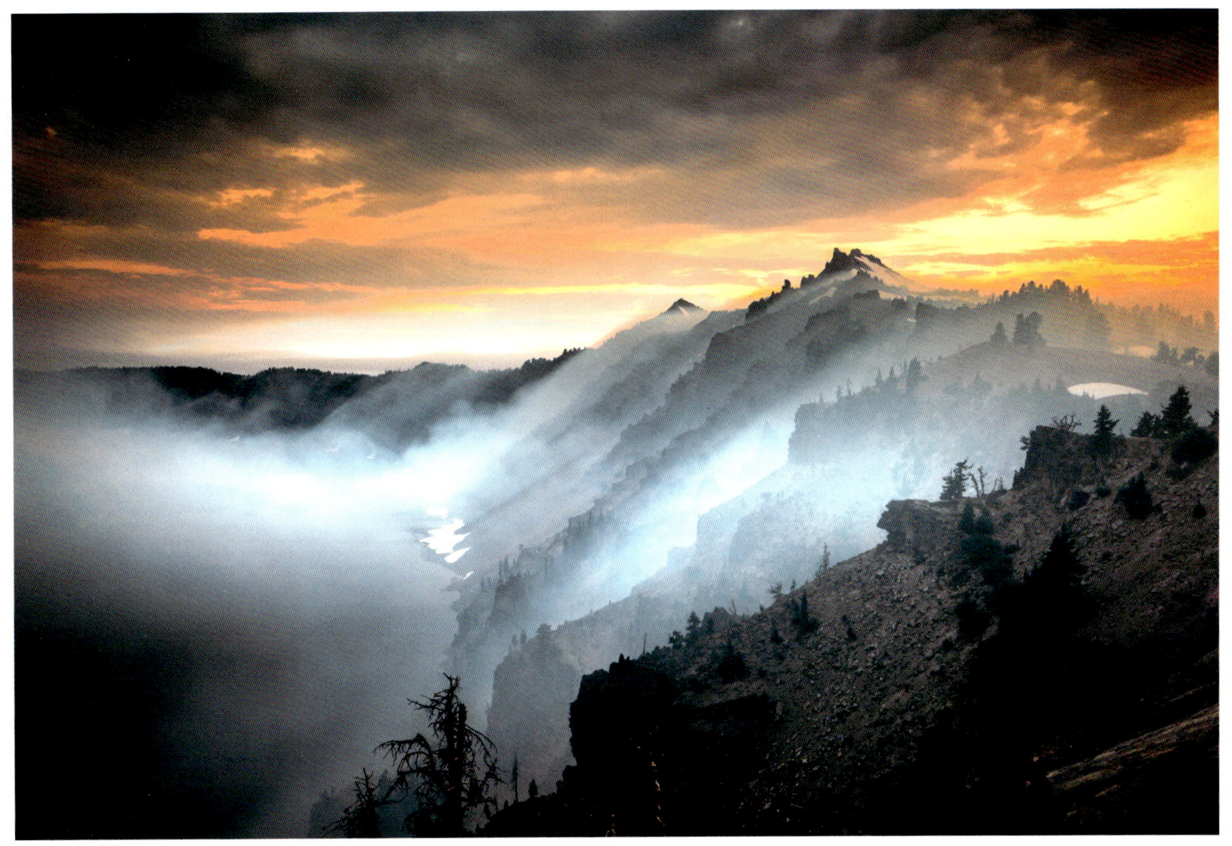

Crater Lake. *Photo by Brandon Herring.*

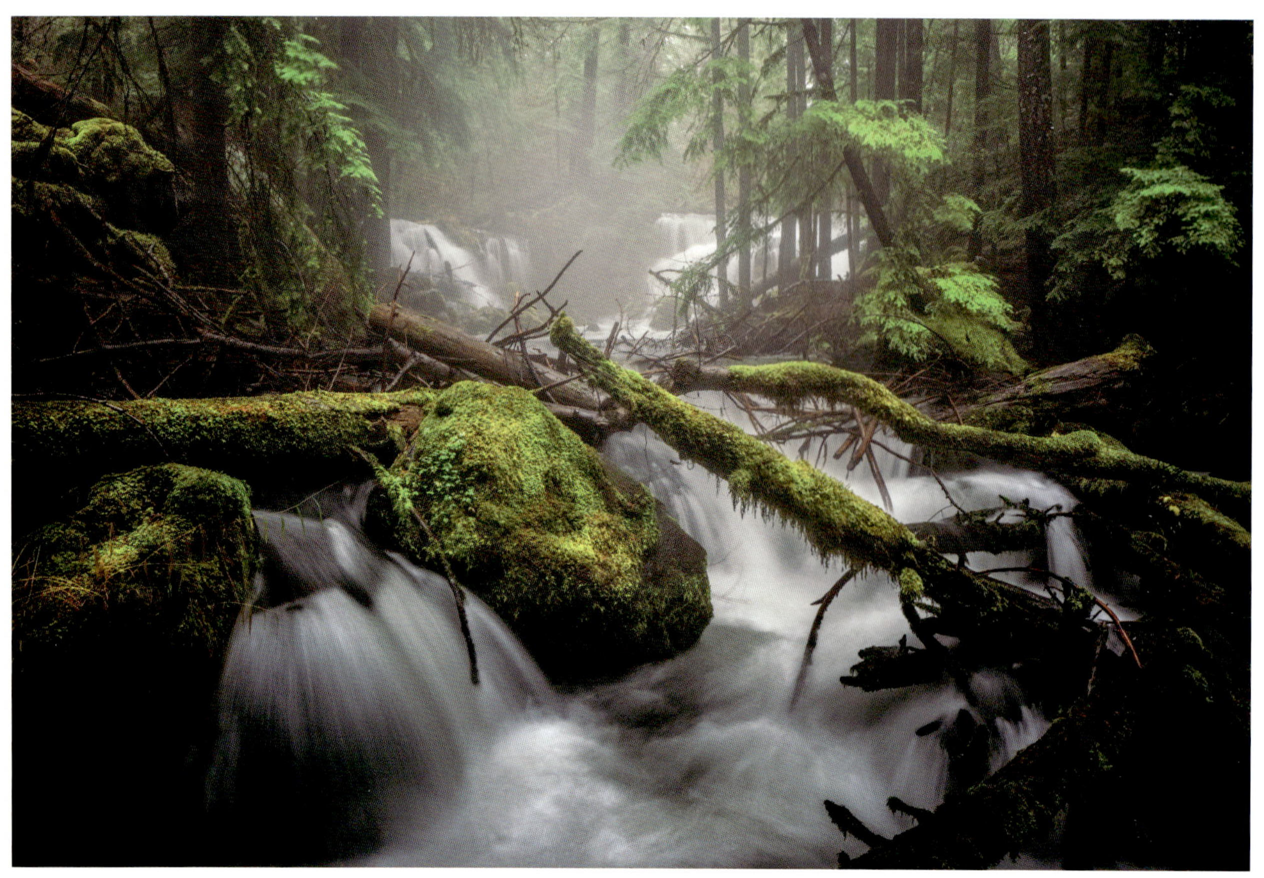

 Pearsony Falls, Prospect. *Photo by Brandon Herring.*

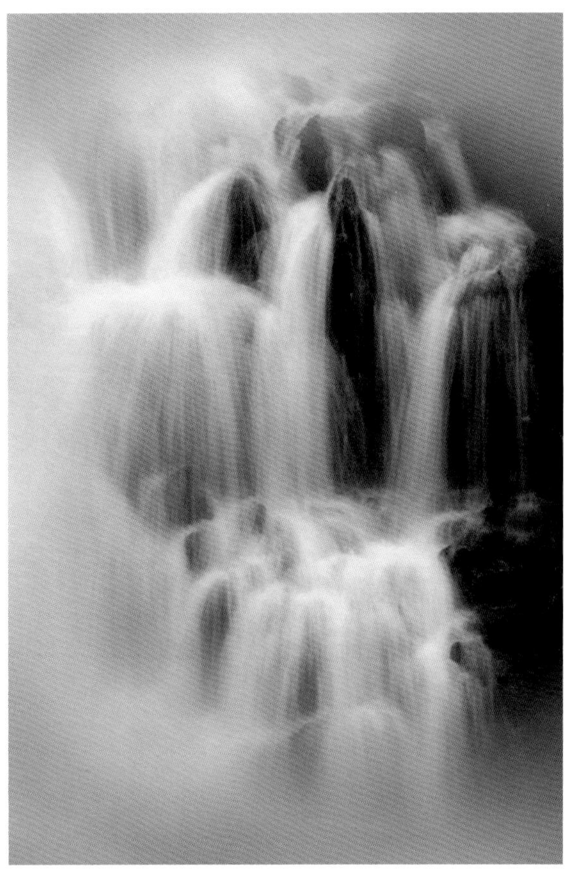

Pearsony Falls, Prospect. *Photo by Julie Bonney.*

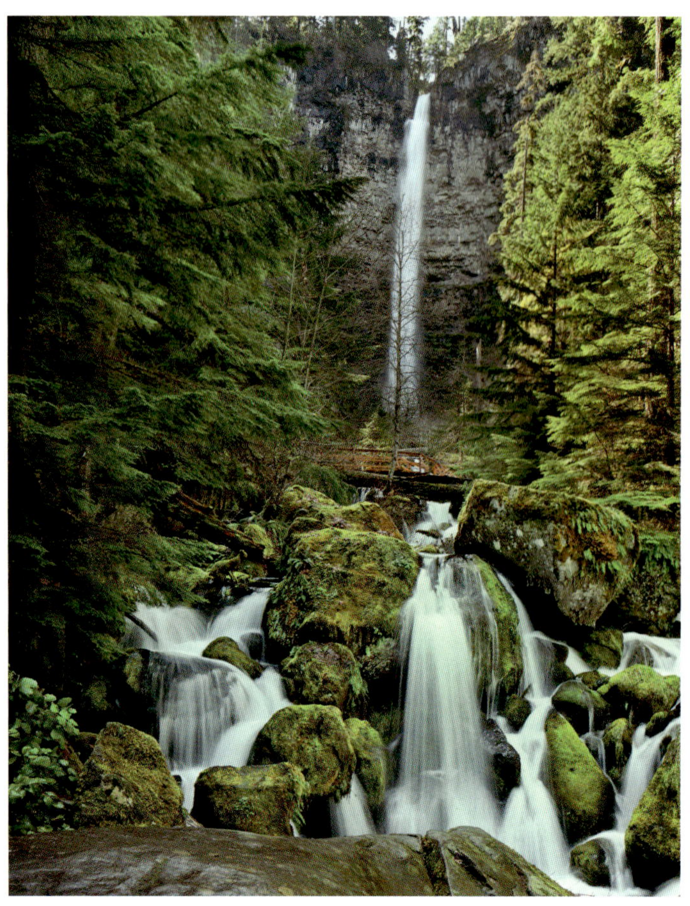

 Watson Falls, Umpqua National Forest. *Photo by John Christer Petersen.*

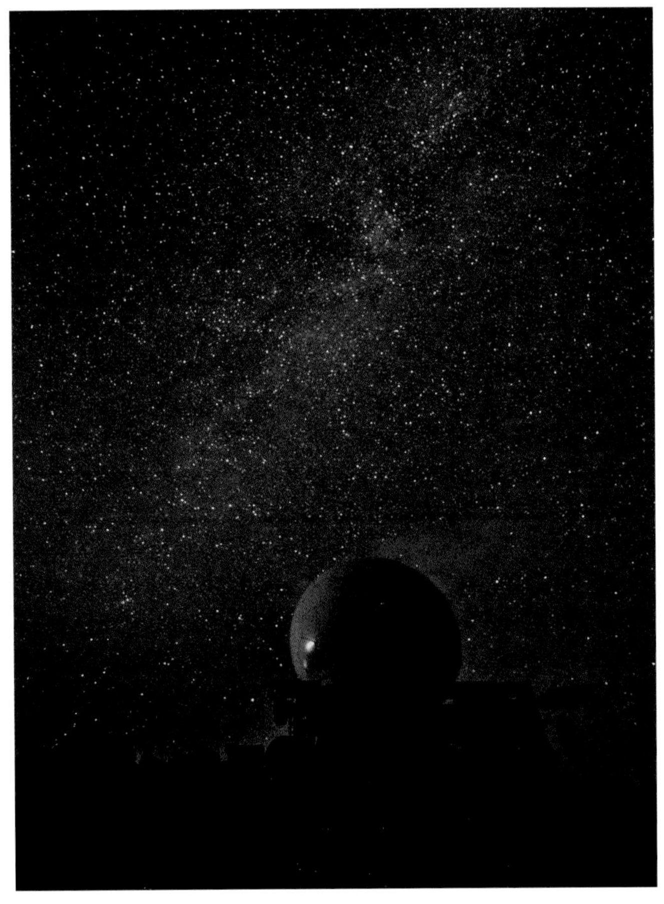

Mount Ashland Radar Sphere and Milky Way. *Photo by Neal R. Thompson.*

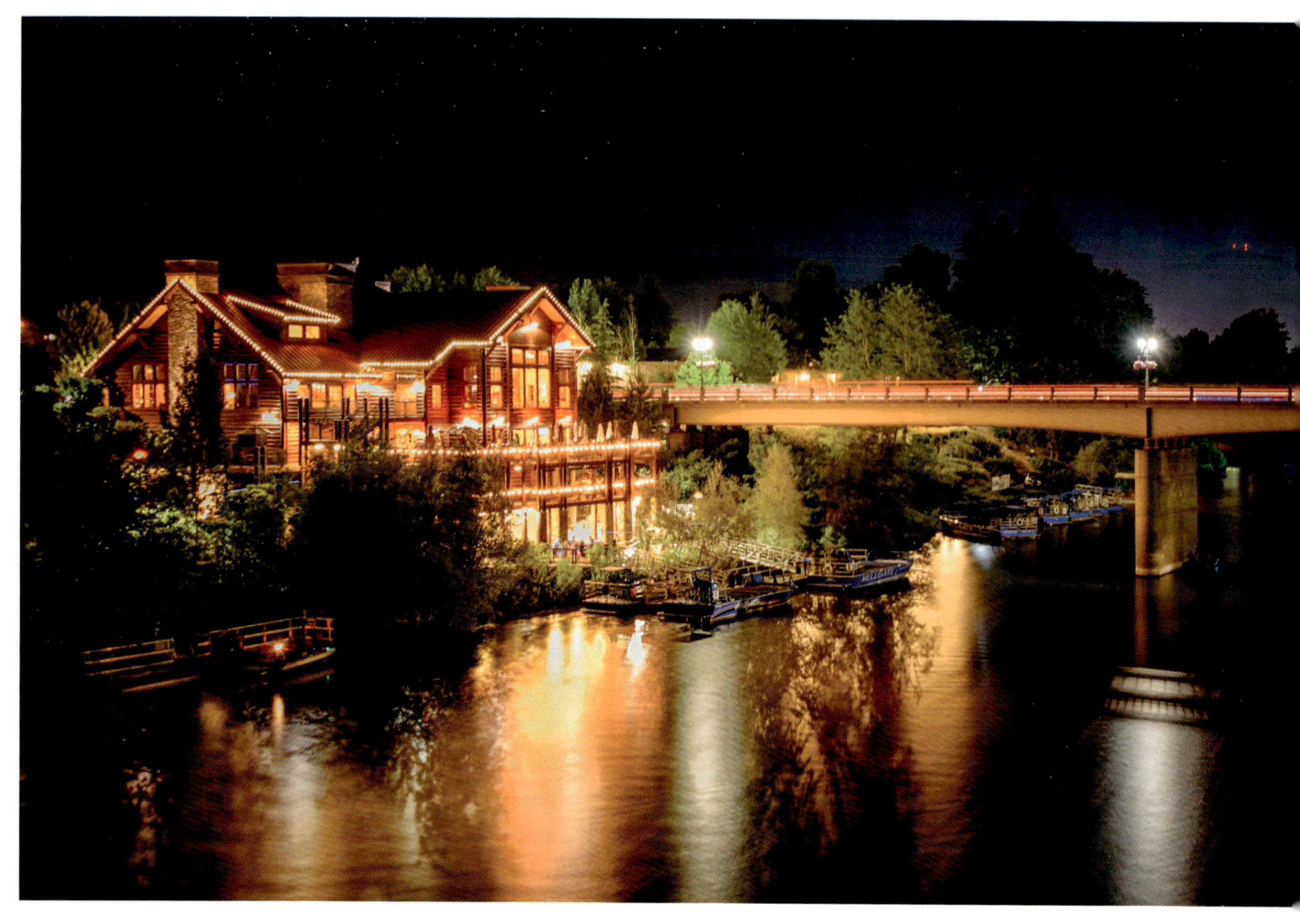

 Rogue River and Taprock Northwest Grill, Grants Pass. *Photo by Nomeca Hartwell.*

CREDITS

The following Oregon photographers contributed to this book.

Sean Bagshaw
Julie Bonney
Randy Bryan
Jim Craven
Ken Deveney
Rudy Dierks
Dan Elster
Terry Fisher
Kate Geary
Nomeca Hartwell
Brandon Herring
Gary Hill
Earshel Hogan
John Kirk
Judy Benson LaNier
Graham Lewis
Cornelius Matteo
Vivian McAleavey
Atana Morell
Jay Newman
Sue Newman
Bob Palermini
Clem Paslack
John Christer Petersen
George F. Peterson
Diana Standing
Alana Lynn Starkweather
Sue Stendebach
Vldn Taylor
Neal R. Thompson
Barbara Tricarico
Nick Viani
Will Volpert
David Lorenz Winston
Matt Witt

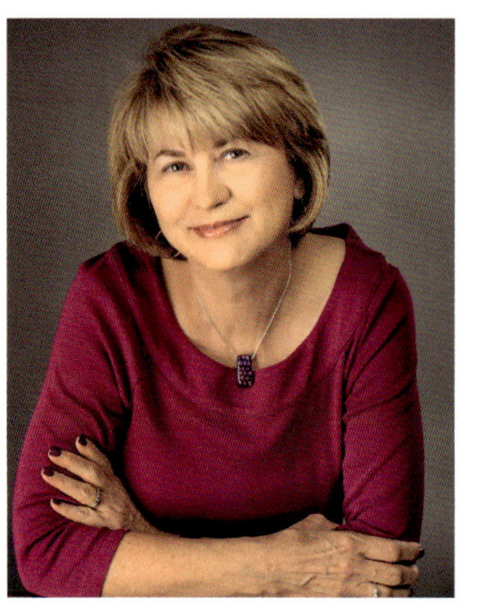

Barbara Tricarico has produced three coffee-table photography books by Schiffer Publishing: *Oregon*; *Ashland, Oregon*; and *Ashland, Oregon, Day Trips*, as well as coauthoring and photographing *Quilts of Virginia: 1607–1899*. She and her husband, Bill, moved to Ashland in 2010. Barbara is an active member of the Ashland Chamber of Commerce, is president of the Southern Oregon Photographic Association, and volunteers for the Ashland Food Project and the Oregon Shakespeare Festival. Barbara enjoys traveling and quilting. Follow her on Facebook at Barbara Tricarico Photography or visit her website, www.barbaratricarico.com.

Photo: Cornelius Matteo